VERMEER
COMPLETE EDITION
PHAIDON

LUDWIG GOLDSCHEIDER

JOHANNES

THE PAINTINGS

WITH INTRODUCTION
CATALOGUE
LIST OF ATTRIBUTIONS
34 COLOUR PLATES AND
83 MONOCHROME
ILLUSTRATIONS

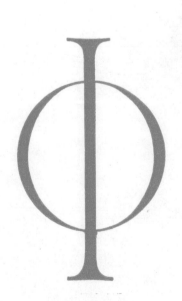

VERMEER

COMPLETE EDITION

PHAIDON PRESS · LONDON

FIRST EDITION 1958
SECOND EDITION 1967

LIST OF CONTENTS

JOHANNES VERMEER

"I am governed by the light —
by shadow you."

Inscription on a sun-dial.

I *Fame*

THE fame of Vermeer is not yet a hundred years old.

During his lifetime he was mentioned only three times in print. The first was when after the explosion of a powder-magazine in Delft in 1654, in which Carel Fabritius lost his life, his printer and publisher Arnold Bon produced a clumsy poem, in which the following verses occur: *So to our loss this Phœnix perished/He departed this life at the height of his fame;/But happily from the ashes there rose once again/Vermeer, who with mastery follows his path.*[1]

The second mention of him is in Bleysweyck's *Description of Delft*, 1667; but only his name is given without praise or blame or reference to any of his works.

A painting by Vermeer, described very generically as "containing a single figure", is mentioned by Balthazar de Monconys in the diary of his travels. On 11th August 1663 he had visited Vermeer in his workshop at Delft, apparently on the look-out for cheap pictures.[2] Vermeer had no pictures to show him, or else did not wish to show him any. De Monconys was then taken to a baker's shop,[3] where a Vermeer was on view, an interior with a single figure, priced 300 florins,[4] but in the opinion of the French art collector worth not more than 50 or 60 at the most.

That is all that Vermeer's contemporaries had to say about him.

The history of his fame begins in the year 1866, with the three illustrated articles which Bürger-Thoré devoted to him in the *Gazette des Beaux-Arts*. The three together do not amount to more than 58 pages . . .

Parnassus is a mountain, not of marble but of clouds, and changes its shape after every gust of wind. There dwell the immortals, but their immortality is not altogether certain: it is an eternal ebb and flow. Winckelmann, the wisest art historian of his time, maintained that Michelangelo was a bad sculptor; Voltaire attempted to prove that Shakespeare had little importance; for Burckhardt Rembrandt was not even the best Dutch painter. Whom did these critics consider to be the greatest of all artists and poets, if they excluded Michelangelo, Shakespeare and Rembrandt? For whose immortality would they have voted? We think we know better, and it is curious how easy it is for us to give all the names of those entitled to dwell on Parnassus; we have no doubts about the rightness of the latest judgments of art, and we believe that these decisions are irrevocable.

It was Bürger-Thoré who brought Vermeer to Parnassus.[5] His three articles were full of enthusiasm, and moreover so penetrating and persuasive, that one cannot help wondering why, before that time, this magical Master had been ranked with prosily capable minor artists like Mieris and Metsu. Nevertheless, another twenty years or so were to pass before Vermeer was generally recognized as "the bird of paradise in the farmyard of Dutch painting".

When in 1874 Jacob Burckhardt delivered his three lectures "On Netherlandish genre-painting", he remarked that in his "Schouburgh" Houbraken had passed over Hobbema and Hooch in silence; but Burckhardt did not notice that Houbraken had also forgotten Vermeer; he deprecated "*the overrated single figures of the Delft painter Meer: women reading and writing letters and such things*"; on the other hand he praised as Vermeer's best work the "Family Group" in the Academy at Vienna (which in reality is by Pieter de Hooch), and in this very connection spoke of the "*magic, by which Van der Meer compels us to share the life of his scenes.*"[6] In his *Maîtres d'autrefois* of 1876 Fromentin has little to say of Vermeer, except that even to his fellow-countrymen this painter appeared an oddity ("*il a des côtés d'observateur assez étranges*") and that in France he was practically unknown (this was ten years after Bürger-Thoré's articles, which Fromentin had obviously never read). Yet a few pages later he mentions a young painter inspired by Vermeer without naming him; presumably he was referring to Pissarro). Fromentin says that the drawings, etching and paintings by this gifted artist, whom he does not name, reveal the influence of Vermeer rather than that of Jacob van Ruisdael. French painters were beginning to discover Vermeer.

Three years later Vermeer's fellow-countryman Van Gogh wrote to his friend Bernard about Vermeer's *Woman in blue reading* in the museum at Amsterdam: "Do you know a painter called Jan van der Meer? He has painted a dignified and beautiful Dutch woman, who is pregnant. The palette of this strange artist comprises blue, lemon-yellow, pearl-grey, black and white. It is true that in the few pictures he painted one can find the whole gamut of colours. But the combination of lemon-yellow, a dull blue and a light grey is as characteristic of him as the harmony of black, white and pink is of Velazquez. The Dutch had no imagination, but they had extraordinary taste and an infallible feeling for composition."[7]

Van Gogh certainly understood the quality of Vermeer; but a few years later a certain Des Tombe, at an auction-sale in The Hague, had to pay only two florins and thirty cents (four shillings and 6d.) for what is perhaps Vermeer's most beautiful picture – *Head of a Girl with pearl ear-drops* – less than was asked for a reproduction of a picture by Meissonier, Millais or Makart. Nevertheless, as early as 1889, one of Vermeer's weaker pictures fetched 75,000 francs at a Paris auction.

The appreciation of Vermeer's art had its origins in France. Zola's *Mon Salon* dedicated to Cézanne appeared in the same year as Bürger-Thoré's articles on Vermeer; and the first high prices for paintings by Vermeer were paid at the time when the poet Verhaeren was beginning to admire the Impressionists and when Durand–Ruel had his first great success with an exhibition in New York of works by French Impressionist painters.

Vermeer became fashionable at the same time as the Impressionists; they had had to wait twenty years, he two hundred.

II *Constellation*

VERMEER was born at Delft, in Holland, in 1632 (in the same year as Luca Giordano and Nicolaes Maes, Spinoza, John Locke and the microbe-hunter Leeuwenhoek). Into what sort of a world was he born?

It was in the middle of the Thirty Years' War. It was the year in which Gustavus Adolphus and Tilly died on the battlefield; but in Holland there was peace. In the heart of Europe cities and pyres

Fig. 1. Jacob van Loo: *Mother and Child* (detail). About 1650. Berlin, Museum.

Fig. 2. Jacopo de' Barbari: *A Sparrowhawk*. About 1512.
London, National Gallery.

Fig. 3. Carel Fabritius: *A Goldfinch*. 1654.
The Hague, Mauritshuis.

Fig. 4. Hendrick van der Burch and Johannes Vermeer: *A Dutch Interior*. About 1649–54.
Tegernsee (near Munich), Princess Editha of Bavaria.

were burning; the armies were marching and brought with them famine, rape, murder and plague. The world was reduced to desperation, but not art. In the year of Vermeer's birth Callot was making his designs for his *Misères de la Guerre*; Rubens had just finished his best religious painting, the St Ildefonso triptych, Rembrandt his *The Anatomy Lesson of Professor Nicolaes Tulp;* Velazquez was painting portraits of King Philip and Prince Baltasar; Bernini, the chief architect of St. Peter's, had almost completed his "Baldacchino"; Poussin was painting his mythologies in Rome; Van Dyck emigrated to England and became court painter to King Charles I.

It was the period of wars of religion; but in Holland several religions and hundreds of sects lived peaceably side by side. There were Remonstrants, Collegiants, Epicurists, Pelagians, Socinians, Rosicrucians, Pantheists, Papists, Antitrinitarians and three groups of Mennonites. Calvinism was the predominating, but not the State religion. From 1610 on, there were no more witches and magicians in Holland, and nobody in that country was burnt.[8] The North was Protestant, the South Catholic; there were differences of opinion, but no murderous hatred. In that country and at that time, as Huizinga has pointed out, the bells tolled only for funerals; the organ was regarded with suspicion, but its voice was so beautiful that the Calvinists did not dare to silence it. Even in the synagogues, Hebrew hymns could be sung without disturbance.

It was an age of reason, with Kepler and Galilei, Descartes and Comenius at its beginning and Leibniz and Newton at its end.[9] And yet it was a period of profound and pure devoutness. For the first time since the Middle Ages genuinely religious pictures were painted; above all by Rembrandt and Zurbarán. Milton, the "genius of Puritanism", Bunyan, the "pilgrim to spiritual eternity", Calderón, the author of almost a hundred Corpus Christi plays, Pascal, the thinker of Port-Royal (where the task which had been set was to "restore religion in its austerity and Christianity in its purity"), Bossuet and Fénelon – all of these wrote their poems, their thoughts, plays and sermons during the two decades in which Vermeer painted his pictures. But mysticism continued to flourish; at that time Jacob Böhme was highly esteemed in Holland and the first collected edition of his writings was published in Amsterdam (1620 and 1682).

In the Protestant provinces of the Netherlands the painting of the younger generation of artists round about 1650 remained rationalistic and realistic. Portraits, landscapes and genre-subjects were their chief themes. The art of Vermeer was borne along in the rationalistic stream of his time, and was never touched at all by the mystical influences.[10]

III *Background*

IN those days Holland consisted of seven provinces, and each of these provinces had its large towns, and each town its local school of painting. Until the middle of the seventeenth century the school of Delft was of no particular importance, but the situation changed abruptly when Carel Fabritius, Paulus Potter, Pieter van Hooch and Jan Steen moved to this wealthy town of breweries and majolica factories.[11] Among the painters born in Delft, the best were Leonard Bramer, Anthonie Palamadesz and Michiel van Miereveld. Bramer had been in Italy and France, was an admirer of Elsheimer and painted landscapes and biblical scenes with small figures; Palamadesz produced pleasing portraits and pretty society pieces; Miereveld, who for a time was court painter to the

Princes of Orange, was very popular among the prosperous burghers of the town on account of his expensive and solid portraits.

The first news of Vermeer's existence is provided by the register of births of the New Church in Delft, under the date of 31 October 1632. The child was baptized *Joannes* (not Jan, as he is usually called[12]). The father, Reynier Janszoon Vos, alias van der Meer or Vermeer, was a burgher of Delft; the mother, Dignum Balthasars or Balten, came from Amsterdam.

Vermeer's father had several trades. He was a silk-weaver and produced "Caffa", a material used mainly for curtains and furniture-coverings; in addition to this he was an art-dealer and a member of the guild of St Luke; lastly he ran a tavern.[13] In his home and tavern called "Mechelen" on the market square in Delft he resided with his family: his wife Dignum, also known as Dymphna, his daughter Geertruyt and his son Johannes, born when his parents had been married for seventeen years, their second and last child.

It would seem that Vermeer's father lived in an atmosphere such as is known to us from paintings by Brower and Steen. An early document informs us that in the course of a brawl in the "Mechelen tavern" Reynier Vermeer, with the help of some of his cronies, beat up a young cadet. Reynier Vermeer was charged with inflicting grievous bodily harm and had to purchase his freedom by paying the doctor's bill and smart-money and standing the cadet and his friends a free dinner.

We do not know in what manner mine host of the "Mechelen" conducted his business as an art-dealer; it may be that exhibitions of pictures were conceived as a means of attracting customers to the tavern. But it is quite probable that after the death of his father Jan Vermeer took over this side of the business and made it his chief source of income.[14] There is no document in existence showing that he ever sold any of his pictures during his lifetime; whenever we hear of any transactions regarding his pictures, it is only as deposits with bakers and provisions-dealers for unpaid bills.[15]

The paternal art-dealer's business was established in 1631. Jan Vermeer married in April 1653, eight months before he became a master and thus acquired the right to sell his work. Two years later his father died, leaving him the house, the tavern and the art-dealer's business; Vermeer had to provide for his mother, his wife, his children and himself. During the last years of his life he seems to have lived on his trade in works of art, for when, after his premature death, his widow declared herself bankrupt, she gave as the only reason for her insolvency the fact that owing to the war the sale of works of art had become difficult. "During the war with the King of France," she said, "my husband earned practically nothing and was forced to sell at a great loss works of art which he had purchased and intended to sell."[16] But not a word about Vermeer's own works.

Vermeer also acted as an expert in matters of art.[17] In 1671 one of the most reputable art-dealers in Amsterdam, Gerrit Uylenburgh, sold thirteen paintings to the Elector of Brandenburg for 30,000 florins; an artist who was asked to give his opinion of them stated that, with one exception, they were "clumsy copies and trash", and the pictures were sent back to Amsterdam. Uylenburgh found experts who were on his side, but others gave unfavourable opinions. The paintings were brought to The Hague, where Vermeer and another Delft painter, Hans Jordaens, were asked to assess their value. They declared that all the works were "*not only not important Italian paintings, but on the contrary undeserving of the names of good masters, and in no case by the great masters to whom they were attributed, and therefore worthless."*[18]

It would appear that Vermeer was not at any period of his life in flourishing circumstances, but thanks to his activity as an art-dealer, he was able to give free rein to his ideas as a painter, without having to make compromises or worry about the possibility of selling his works. At the time of his death – if I have read the documents correctly – most of his paintings were still in the possession of the family.[19]

IV *Life and Work*

AFTER priming the background of the picture of Vermeer's life and inserting a few strokes and shadings, we come to the figure of the man itself, and it is here that our difficulties begin; for though it would be easy enough to add to the background, the figure remains vague, and only when we turn away from it and examine the works, can we obtain some insight into Vermeer's real being.

The documents, of which a great number have been preserved, do not tell us anything very important about him; from them we learn that he was baptized on 31 October 1632, married on 5 April 1653 and received into the guild of St Luke on 29 December of the same year; they also tell us that he was twice elected to the committee of the guild (1662–1663 and 1669–1670) and give details of various small legacies and money transactions, of a thousand florins which his mother-in-law had to lend him and which he never paid back, and finally of his death on 15 December 1675 at the age of 43. We also learn that he left a widow with eight children under age, in addition to three who were already adults, and we are told of his numerous debts and of the precarious state of his art-dealer's business.

Of Vermeer the artist we learn nothing at all from the documents, not even where and under whom he learned to paint. Since the period of apprenticeship in Holland at that time was six years and Vermeer became a master in 1653, he must have begun his apprenticeship by 1647 at the latest. But under whom?[20]

Swillens suggested Leonard Bramer. "*The family Bramer were good friends of the Vermeers. This is also shown by the drawings which Leonard Bramer drew from paintings of different masters – now collected in the so-called 'Sketchbook of Leonard Bramer' in the Print Room at Amsterdam – amongst which there were also one or more pieces which were in the collection of Reynier Vermeer, Johannes' father.*" But there is nothing in Vermeer's youthful, let alone in his later works, that reminds one of Bramer.

It is usually assumed that Carel Fabritius, and not Bramer, was Vermeer's teacher; but Carel Fabritius, who came to Delft about 1650, was not admitted to the guild until 1652, whereas Vermeer, as we have just seen, must have begun his apprenticeship about 1647, and therefore not under Fabritius.[21]

Certain similarities between Vermeer's manner of painting and that of Fabritius prove nothing. Dark figures against a light ground, although not very usual, were not against the taste of the time. We find portraits set against a light ground in the work of Hals and Rembrandt, or even earlier, in that of the Master of Flémalle, Dürer and Lotto. The background of Jacopo de' Barbari's *Falcon* is Fig. 2, 3 not much darker than that of Fabritius' *Goldfinch*; and even Caravaggio once painted a flower-piece against a white wall.[22]

It is not impossible that Vermeer received his first instruction in drawing from his father, who as a silk-weaver probably designed his own flower and figure patterns for curtains, and that the young artist then continued his training in the studio of some minor Delft painter. Here we are entering the field of conjecture, but in order to leave nothing unsaid, I would like to mention Hendrick van der Burch, who was a member of the Delft painters' guild from 1649 to 1654, and, though he was no great master, was a very original artist whose works have often been attributed to Vermeer, for which reason it was assumed that he must have been influenced by Vermeer. The relationship could, however, have been the reverse, since in 1649 Van der Burch was almost twice as old as Vermeer.[23] If it were possible to assign an exact date to Hendrick van der Burch's *Interior* in the museum of Berlin, or if we at least knew for certain that it was painted during his stay in Delft, then there would be more justification for considering Van der Burch as Vermeer's teacher, rather than Carel Fabritius or Leonard Bramer. (See note on Cat. No. 11, p. 127.)

Nevertheless, the fact remains that Bramer acted as witness when Vermeer married Catharina Bolnes at the town hall in Delft on 5 April 1653. At the time Vermeer was twenty-one years and six months old, and Catharina twenty-two. She and her mother,[24] as we can see from a number of documents, were competent women who knew how to deal with financial matters; during Vermeer's last years, and also after his death, the two women entered into ingenious contracts with a view to freeing the family property, and subsequently Vermeer's estate, from a crushing burden of debt. Catharina would also seem to have been quite good-looking, if we are justified in identifying her as the original of a number of attractive female figures in Vermeer's pictures.

That Vermeer used his wife as a model, just as Rembrandt, Terborch and other painters of the time chose their models from among their family circles, can hardly be doubted. E. V. Lucas (1922) and Bodkin (1940) have put forward the interesting supposition that the woman in Vermeer's *Woman in blue reading a letter* is a portrait of Catharina during one of her numerous pregnancies. According to Malraux, the woman dressed in yellow in the Dresden picture of 1656 is painted from the same model, as well as the *Sleeping Girl* and the *Lady reading a letter at an open window*, if we judge the similarity by the reflection in the glass pane of the window. But in genre-pictures the question of similarity is not of great importance and one could go even further and conclude that probably the kneeling nymph in the Hague *Diana*, who is wearing the same dress as the *Sleeping Girl*, and even the laughing young woman in the painting in the Frick collection, who is dressed in exactly the same way as the *Lady reading* in Dresden, all reproduce the same model, namely Vermeer's wife. To these must be added the Mary in the Edinburgh picture and perhaps also the *Lady weighing pearls*.

We have no letters written by Vermeer, not a single page from a diary, not even a note or a line concerning his relations with his wife, his family, his friends and his enemies, nothing whatsoever that can give us even the shadowiest insight into his life. All we can do to satisfy our curiosity is examine his pictures and abandon ourselves to speculations, but even these are based on nothing but the supposed identity of models. Yet we can perhaps interpret paintings like dreams, which after all are made of the same stuff.

The most mysterious and at the same time the easiest of these pictures to interpret is *At the Procuress*, painted three years after Vermeer's marriage.[25]

In the upper half of this picture four personages are shown in half-length; the lower part of the

Fig. 5. Hendrick van der Burch: *A Dutch Interior*. About 1649–54. Berlin, Museum.

Fig. 6. Cornelis de Man: *Three Geographers* (detail). About 1660. Hamburg, Kunsthalle.

Figs. 7 and 8. Jan van der Meer of Utrecht: Man drinking wine; Boy eating pods. Signed and dated 1656. Warsaw, National Museum.

painting is occupied by a barrier – a table over which a cloak and a Turkish rug have been thrown.[26]

The composition is obviously closely related to representations of the Prodigal Son in a house of ill fame. Would Vermeer have used his wife as a model for such a picture?

Rembrandt, shortly after his marriage, once painted himself with sword and beer-glass, with the beautiful Saskia on his lap, in a crude picture the motive of which, as Carl Neumann has said, "occurs elsewhere in Dutch art only as a brothel motive".[27] Nevertheless, in Rembrandt's picture of drunkenness and love, the lover is Rembrandt himself; he is merely drinking to the health of the spectator and making him a witness of the scene.

In Vermeer's *At the Procuress* his wife is the prostitute. She is the lightest and the most beautiful figure in the picture, with the careful gradation of shades in her yellow jacket, her dark wide eyelids, her red mouth, her gently outstretched hand and her head-dress radiating light. The musician in the left upper corner is, as René Gimpel was the first to point out,[28] a self-portrait of Vermeer. The richly contrasted modelling of the head is a reminiscence of one of Rembrandt's self-portraits.) Fig. 12 Both the man and the woman hold wine-glasses in their hands, while the woman smiles and the man grins; in front of him, on the barrier, hangs his shaggy fur-lined cloak, as black as a pall, and in front of the girl the rug forms a large, brightly coloured patch; the yellow of her jacket appears again very faintly round the self-portrait. Between the musician and the courtesan, who are placed as far away from each other as possible, stand the bawd and the soldier. Who was the model for the bawd? Vermeer's mother-in-law? And who was the model for the young soldier with his fleshy hand? Is the picture an expression of jealousy, fear or hatred? Or was it born in the dark depths of the soul, where dreams and visions dispose of realities freely and irresponsibly?

The picture is of an ingenious and almost brutal originality, which Vermeer never repeated afterwards.

In the *Sleeping Girl* the same model is used as in the painting we have just discussed. Once again the foreground is occupied by a barrier covered with a rug terminated on the right by the back of a chair. The background is relieved by a glimpse into an adjoining room (a motive of which Pieter de Hooch was fond). The colouring of the picture is dark and severe, almost mournful; above the head of the girl hangs a heavy shadow. The motive of the seated figure with the elbow propped on the table, and the head resting against the upraised hand is very old indeed; it goes back to Greek figures on tombs, to Gothic miniatures, to Dürer and Signorelli.[29] This figure is a personification of grief. In the *Sleeping Girl* it symbolizes the sorrows of love, as can be seen from the picture hanging in the room and partly visible in the upper left corner.[30] This picture within a picture represents the God of Love, with a bow in his right hand and a letter in his left, but here Vermeer adds on his own initiative a cast-off mask, which lies on the ground at the God's feet.[31] Such masks are to be seen especially in the works of Michelangelo, for example in the pictures of *Venus and Cupid* and *The Dream of Human Life* painted after his cartoons, where they signify deception, disappointment and also the frustration brought about by love and the unreality of all pleasure. The mask of Michelangelo's *Night* symbolizes the "phantoms of dreams".

The mask in Vermeer's *Sleeping Girl* is interpreted by Swillens as "Love Unmasked", or "Disillusioned and Disappointed Love".[32] According to Gowing it denotes "a fantasy of love" or perhaps also sleep as "the discarding of a mask".[33]

In any case the theme is a peculiar one, and still more peculiar is the fact that Vermeer should have used his wife as a model for this allegory of sensual dreamlife. It is as if he wanted to reveal her innermost thoughts, in whatever way we choose to interpret the symbolism.

In the large painting in The Hague the same figure in the same dress is kneeling before Diana the Goddess of chastity and washing her feet – a very humble role.

5 This picture seems to be filled with a passion which is expressed through the colours. From the centre of the painting, a sweeping yellow drapery, a deep orange-red like a flame, leads diagonally to the upper left corner, where a few dark-gold patches of light in the foliage repeat the colour of the centre. In the heart of the picture, like the edge of a fire, gleams a sharp blue, shading off into a blackish blue and repeated more faintly in the top right corner by the blue of the sky. In addition we have purple and golden-brown, the red of faded roses and dark flesh-tones; all against a ground of heavy green, which makes the vigorous colours more brilliant.

Vermeer's only religious painting, and certainly the earliest of all his works, *Christ in the house of* 1 *Mary and Martha*, was still based on red and dark-blue, in the style of Caravaggio; *Diana and her* 5 *Companions*, Vermeer's only composition showing figures in a landscape, is different, for it is Venetian in its glowing colours. In both paintings the corner figures, for which we assume that Catharina Vermeer was the model, occupy the lowest position in the picture.[34]

16 Was Catharina also the model for the *Lady reading a letter* in Dresden?

Letters play an important part in Vermeer's paintings. Time and again he painted women reading or writing letters, receiving a letter or handing one to a maid for dispatch. Twice Cupid appears with a letter in his hand (according to Swillens this symbolizes a proposal of love). All these women writing or reading letters are confined as if in caverns and shut off from the world. This is particularly noticeable in the Dresden picture: in the foreground there is the barrier of a table covered with a rug (the dish of apples and the folds of the rug form a rising barrier): on the right there is a curtain which looks as if it were cast in bronze; above is the room itself with its shadows. The dull green of the picture, in which only the yellow of the dress, the fruit and the sallow flesh stand out, contributes to the impression of isolation. This little figure, lost in the cavernous setting, is standing at an open window, the panes of which reflect her face. A red curtain flutters above the window-opening, that peephole on to the outer world – a moving piece of cloth, like the wing of a bird, sailing slowly through the air. Window and letter, these two things alone link the lonely figure to the outer world. Everything in this picture is petrified, even the curtain has been partially caught by the casement. Motionless, the woman is reading her letter, which has come to her from outside; if she looks up, she will see herself reflected in the pane.

The composition of this painting is derived from those of the Virgin in the chamber, the Virgin of the Annunciation. For example, in Crivelli, the Madonna appears in this way, enclosed within Fig. 13 the setting and with a curtain on the right; and in Grünewald the resemblance is even closer. Vermeer may have found the motive in the works of one of the early Netherlandish masters.

The dress of the woman reading a letter in the Dresden picture is found again in the *Soldier and* 14 *Laughing Girl* in the Frick Collection. Is it merely the same dress, or is it also the same model? This is a cheerful picture. The usual barrier is replaced in the left foreground by the dark-blue back of a chair and by the red and black back of a soldier, while on the right the setting has no termination and

(18)

the eye is barely arrested by a patch of shadow. The figure of the laughing girl, dressed in yellow and blue, is seated before a white wall beneath a bright-coloured map of Holland – the country, the whole world is open to her.

After his marriage, Vermeer and his wife went to live with his parents in the "Mechelen" house on the market square of Delft. The tavern was on the ground-floor and the living quarters on the upper floors. The same building housed the silk-weaving workshop and his father's art-dealer's business. In 1655 the father died, at the age of about sixty. The mother went on living in the house for some time, but then moved into a house of her own in the Vlamingstraat. The reason for this separation is unknown; was it perhaps because she could not get on with her daughter-in-law? In other respects also we know far too little of Vermeer's life. Did he, after his mother's departure, carry on the "Mechelen" tavern with his wife and his increasing tribe of children? If he did, then he could have observed in his own house scenes such as *The Soldier and the Laughing Girl*.

One side of the house looked out on to the Voldersgracht and the municipal home for old people.[35] Standing at one of the windows of his home, Vermeer painted the view of the houses opposite. The *Street in Delft* was thus painted in a room, but is a view of the world outside; in fact it is the earliest of all plein-air paintings. The Dutch landscape-painters must certainly have often worked in the open air, but all their pictures have the values of interiors, and that is true of Rembrandt, Ruisdael, Hobbema and De Hooch. Vermeer is an exception, and even in his interiors he comes very close to plein-air painting, except that his treatment of light invariably has only one direction and we never find diffused light in his pictures. Nor do we find in his works that use of light and shade for purposes of contrast and as expressive values which was so frequent in Baroque painting. Vermeer evolved a simple and ingenious solution: broad daylight; and a modulation of this which, according to whether it contains more or less light, does not define the individual forms everywhere and at every place, but shows how light and objects encounter one another and how they become spatially visible.[36]

Reality as it appears before our eyes is reproduced only on exceptional occasions in a painting. Even photography cannot achieve this, for in the first place the camera sees with only one eye and therefore reproduces a depth which is not stereoscopic – as we see it with our two eyes. And in the second place the camera sees the near and the far away at the same time, whereas we have to adjust the focus of our eyes twice in order to obtain the same sharpness of vision. Moreover, our field of vision is limited, and a painter has to move his head first to one side and then to the other in order to see everything that he includes in the near distance in his picture. By using a convex mirror – Dou, for example, is known to have used such a mirror – this problem is eliminated, for a diminishing glass shows a limited segment which can be viewed at *one* glance. If we look at the objects to be painted through an empty picture-frame and if the differences of depth in the segment from Nature are not great, we can arrive at a limitation similar to that obtained with the aid of a convex mirror; the casement of a window can serve the same purpose.

Vermeer reproduced this view of the street through the framework of a window, from a room on ground level with his eye about three yards above the ground and at a distance of about twelve yards.[37] The effect of depth is weak and seems to be the result of a single focusing. This explains the magical effect produced by this very simple picture, for it is thus that we really see things.

(19)

The composition of the picture is based solely on the choice of the excerpt and on the "arrangement" of the colours.

It is questionable to what an extent the colours of this painting have changed in the course of three hundred years. I do not believe that they have changed very much, and if they have changed at all, it has certainly not been to their disadvantage. Undoubtedly they have become darker, in particular the white. The blue has certainly "grown through". That means that in the green tones, especially in the foliage, the yellow lake has disappeared and the ultramarine has become independent. It may be, however, that Vermeer foresaw this change. (Ingres, for example, painted his shadows in violet, because he knew that in the course of time they would change to a warm brown.) In any case, in Vermeer's *Street in Delft* the blue-tipped foliage has a special charm, just as the blue trees have in the *View of Delft*, the only other landscape by his hand.[38] The vigorous blue of the dress of the woman standing in the passage in the *Street*, brilliant as a sapphire, gives exactly the right amount of accentuation to the lower extremity of the V-shaped composition. In the colours of the water in the *View of Delft*, however, the blue does not manage to free itself from the brown tones, nor has it come through the clouds of the blue sky; only the foliage gleams in this picture, like an embroidery consisting of blue glass beads.

This view of Delft is Vermeer's homage to his native city. It is a convincingly faithful portrait; not a stone nor a leaf has been overlooked; no other town in the world has ever been so lovingly depicted. We need only compare Vermeer's painting with the most famous townscapes of the Baroque in order to see how Vermeer keeps clear of all "stage effects". El Greco's *Toledo* and Ruisdael's *Village of Egmond* are pathetic paraphrases; the *View of Saragossa* by Mazo and Velazquez is just a large frieze of figures with a town in the background. The views of towns in Venetian and Netherlandish altar-pieces comply with the laws established for accessories in a picture; they have not the sharply characterized individual features which are given to even the least important figures in these compositions. It would also be wrong to compare the little engravings and etchings of towns produced by Merian and Hollar with Vermeer's large view of Delft, for the intention of the former is purely topographical, they are merely prosaic renderings of the position and outline of towns, but not of their souls.[39] Could Vermeer have painted any other town so beautifully? The *View of Delft* is the portrait of the city in which Vermeer was born, lived and died.

To me it seems that more beautiful clouds, more tranquil, profound waters have never been painted than in this picture, that there has never been a more fluctuating reflection, or such perceptible air. Nevertheless it is clear that this landscape with its simple perfection did not always meet with appreciation. Jozef Israels and Wilson Steer considered it not remarkable.[40]

Another Vermeer painting which has baffled many critics is the *Milkmaid*. Ever since the days of Reynolds it has been one of the most popular of all Dutch paintings, and the girl has even been considered to be an embodiment of Hollandia. She is a large and serious figure, as monumental as a Greek statue, a sister of Michelangelo's Sibyls. The execution of this picture is most remarkable: the still-life in the foreground is full of sparks of colour (consisting of knots of paint), the arms are painted with a thick impasto, almost sculpturesque, the rest of the painting being comparatively thin. On the right, round the dark outline of the silhouette, runs a white line, like an indication of an irradiation of light. One could call the picture "naturalistic", but that would not mean anything

Fig. 9. Vermeer: *The Lacemaker*. About 1665. Paris, Louvre. – Fig. 10. Velazquez (attributed): *The Needlewoman*. About 1648. Washington, National Gallery of Art (Mellon Collection).

Fig. 11. *Supposed Self-Portrait of Vermeer* (detail from Plate 13). 1656.

Fig. 12. *Rembrandt's Self-Portrait*, 1633. Etching (detail, enlarged).

Fig. 13. Matthias Grünewald: *Virgin of the Annunciation*
(detail, reversed). About 1515. Colmar, Museum.

Fig. 14. Vermeer: *Woman reading in a Room*. About 1658.
Dresden, Gallery.

Fig. 15. Giovanni Biliverti (Jan Bilivelt of Maestricht):
Christ and the Samaritan Woman (detail, reversed). About 1640.
Vienna, Kunsthistorisches Museum (Depot).

Fig. 16. Vermeer: *Detail from Plate 1*. About 1654.
Christ and Martha.
Edinburgh, National Gallery of Scotland.

Fig. 17. Vermeer: *Detail from Plate 41*. About 1663.
Brunswick, Museum.

Fig. 18. Jan Steen: *Music Lesson* (detail). About 1656.
Rotterdam, Museum Boymans (Loan).

Fig. 19. *A mourning Maidservant*. Greek sculpture (detail)
from a tomb in Attica. 4th century B.C. Berlin, Museum.

Fig. 20. Nicolaes Maes: *A sleeping Maidservant* (detail). 1655.
London, National Gallery.

Fig. 21. Leonardo da Vinci: *Drawing*. A man sitting at a "prospettografo" looking at an armillary sphere and drawing it on a glass pane. About 1488. Milan, Ambrosiana (Codex Atlanticus). – Fig. 22. Dürer: *Drawing*. A tracing apparatus consisting of a glass pane and a peep-hole. 1514. Dresden, Print Room. – Fig. 22-A. Dürer: *Detail from the verso of the drawing Fig. 22*. A draughtsman using a tracing apparatus. – Fig. 23. *A portable camera obscura;* from Charles-Antoine Jombert's *Méthode pour apprendre le dessein*. Paris, 1755. – Fig. 24. *A portable camera obscura*, by Robert Hooke, London, 1668. – Fig. 25. *The camera obscura of Joachim Franz Beich, 1715;* detail from a mezzotint engraving by J. J. Haid.

more than saying that it is "Dutch". Plietzsch, who praises it highly, concludes his description by saying: "*There is almost an excess of brilliant technique. One feels that the illusory rendering is a trifle inartistic.*" M. J. Friedländer would also seem to have been thinking of this painting of Vermeer's when he wrote: "*In this artistic effort one detects a spiritual poverty and an echo of photography and wax-work shows and there are times when we prefer other Dutch painters to him on account of their ingenuousness.*"

Reynolds, with the keen glance of a creative artist, perceived the real reason for this resemblance to "photography and waxworks shows"; during his journey to Holland (when he saw the *Milkmaid*) he wrote to a friend: "Dutch pictures are a representation of nature, just as it is seen in a camera obscura."[41]

Reynolds himself used the camera for some of his portraits,[42] and he was right in noticing that Vermeer had used it too. The influence which this had on the perspective in his paintings, on the sharpness of the outlines and on the distribution of the high lights, has been discussed by Hyatt Mayor (who quoted Allyn Cox) and subsequently by L. Gowing.[43]

From the earliest times artists normally made use of mechanical aids on a far greater scale than is generally supposed; workshop appliances from the simplest to the most complicated: reticulated frames, flat and convex mirrors, drawing apparatuses, cameragraphs, etc. Sculptors from Thutmosis to Riccio used casts from Nature, Leonardo da Vinci, Dürer and Holbein worked with the aid of a tracing-apparatus; and ever since Giovanni Battista della Porta had first described the camera obscura (1558), it had been commonly used in the studios of painters. Zanetti tells us that Canaletto used it to obtain correct architectural perspective. Nor did more modern artists disdain such aids: Constable and Sickert used the tracing-apparatus, Hodler the camera obscura, Manet and Degas the photographic camera.[44]

Figs. 21, 22

A reproduction of a camera obscura of Vermeer's time has come down to us, namely that of a portable camera such as could be used when drawing landscapes. Robert Hooke, who designed this camera and described it in 1668, was in correspondence with Anthony van Leeuwenhoek, the Delft naturalist; it is probable that Vermeer knew Leeuwenhoek.[45]

Fig. 24

In a statement dating from about 1700 we are told that "Several Dutch painters are said to have studied and imitated, in their paintings, the effect of the camera obscura and its manner of showing nature. . . . The effect of the camera is striking but false."[46]

For creative artists the camera is dangerous not so much because it tempts them to reproduce the perspectival distortion and alienation of objects, but because it makes Nature a mere semblance and the artist himself only a mirror. The world of forms becomes more and more independent, the reflected images absorb all life, and the personality of the creator disappears. Works of art thus become purer and more formal, and cold as crystal.

If an artist is prepared to content himself with the casual content of phenomena – if he looks at the world with the eyes of a camera – then his creative activity is reduced to the moulding of form: pure technique acquires great importance and he can find pleasure and fulfilment only in the perfection and beauty with which he endows the phenomenon represented. The smoothness of the surface in Vermeer's paintings was created in exactly the same way as the smoothness of the phrases of Flaubert and other exponents of pure artistry. In the artist's vision of the world art is not just a coloured reflection of life, but a more logical and satisfying, an imperishable reality, as absolute and abstract as mathematics. Form becomes an interpretation of life. "One cannot be an artist," says Nietzsche, "without paying the penalty of conceiving as *contents*, as the matter itself, what the non-artist calls *form*. This means that the artist belongs to an upside-down world, for content now seems to be something merely formal – including his own life." [47]

The works which Vermeer painted during the last twelve years of his career show the progress of this cooling-off (or, if we like to call it so, crystallization). Time after time these pictures have been considered as "queer" – Fromentin was the first to describe this feeling; and yet it is difficult to understand this impression of strangeness, because after all Vermeer "kept so close to Nature". These paintings seem strange and weird because in them form has become content, because their beauty is only skin-deep. Vermeer, the antithesis of Rembrandt, had no message to proclaim, except that of the beauty of coloured surfaces, "the deeds of light". (This limitation gives rise to an uncompromising strength and an uncanny talent for achieving perfection.) His view of the world was that of an artist; for him, as an absolute artist, reality and his own life were "purely matters of form".

His manner of painting became smooth and enamel-like. Visible brushstrokes, showing how the picture is created stroke by stroke, are the signature of an ego-conscious creator: in the finished picture we can still see the painter at work. That was how Titian and Rembrandt[48] painted, Tintoretto and El Greco, Frans Hals and the Impressionists. Vermeer did not paint with his whole arm, but with his fingers: his pictures are smooth and perfectly finished and do not reveal how they were created. Even Vermeer's earlier pictures have a noble leanness; his last works go still further in this direction, becoming not lifeless, but wintry: just as mountains and trees bare their skeletons, so do Vermeer's late figure-compositions reveal their geometrical construction.

5, 18, 27 In his early period he had painted three pictures set in the open air; all the rest are interiors. In most cases the figures are set in front of a light-coloured wall;[49] only in one picture and for the heads 66, 54, 76 of two women did Vermeer prefer dark curtains as ground. The earliest of his interiors still look very harmless; one can compare them with De Hooch and Terborch. But they seem to be filled with a tremendous stillness, in which only the light crackles. An open casement or a chair indicate the line of vision and the spatial depth; everything is in such careful equilibrium, that the slightest turning would have shattered the whole composition. The figures sit as motionless as puppets. In each of these pictures, one glance is held fast, just as one holds on to one thought. The very fact that they are so motionless, seems to make these pictures eternal. They breathe an infinite tranquillity, even the most trivial objects they contain, these things of glass or wood or cloth, are fixed in the setting and do not change; they are endowed with immortality.

In many of Vermeer's pictures the figures are standing or sitting in the extreme foreground; everything is brought so close to our eyes that we see only the bottoms of the chairs, not the legs; in others, everything is pushed so far into the background that the foreground is "only filled with air".[50]

Vermeer has been called a painter of still-lifes – but in Dutch still-lifes all the objects are continuously and separately modelled, whereas Vermeer, just like a landscape-painter, paints across the forms and constructs his interiors out of near distance, middle distance and far distance. In the foreground there is a barricade without any details, far too close up; bread, fruit and chinaware sparkling with colour as if they were in the open air; the rest is too far away. Van Eyck and the other early Netherlandish artists painted everything too close, for the sake of clarity. Vermeer painted everything in the middle distance too far away, whereby objects lose their identity, their familiar forms.

Even when he brings objects right up into the foreground, he paints them with the blueness of distance. He arranges colours and forms as if he was creating a flower-piece, a decorative coloured composition; but then he modulates without regard for the individual forms, in the same way in which light flows. The pattern of his pictures evolves like the melody on an Aeolian harp; in Vermeer's works everything appears to have been carefully calculated, but is nevertheless determined by the casual vision which he saw in his camera. From the camera Vermeer also derived the vagueness of the nearest portions and the mellow focus of the middle distance rich in details: with him the light dissolves the phenomena to the point of making tangible things unrecognizable and obliterating the boundaries between objects.

Vermeer's art is an art of vision, not of invention; an art of painting, not of composition. In his works, as in those of the old dramatists, the derivation of the motives is of no importance. To quote one example (to the exclusion of others) he derived from Jan Steen the motive of a thinking or dozing man with his arm supporting his head. For Jan Steen too, this figure represents an indifferent, Fig. 18 isolated spectator of a scene, calculated to excite the interest of those who see the picture. But what does Vermeer make out of this figure; Even the napkin underneath the jug has more expression 41 and more "painterly" grandeur than the most successful heads of Steen. (Only Cézanne, two hundred years later, understood how to endow such white, folded cloths with so much monumentality and significance.) Amidst the grey realism of Dutch painting, the coloured, tranquil art of Vermeer is like a rainbow which stands in a cloudy sky and alters the appearance of everything.

It is just as easy to find all Vermeer's accessories in works of his painter contemporaries, as it is to discover that in his pictures everything is different. About 1660 pearl ear-drops were very much the fashion in Holland; we find them in the female portraits and genre-pieces of Terborch, Metsu, Mieris and many other artists. But with Vermeer these large, drop-shaped, gleaming pearls become the points of convergence of the light, symbols of the beauty of the world. (It would seem that later generations did not always approve of Vermeer's pearls, for in one case a large pearl of this kind was overpainted and replaced by an ornamental gold ear-drop.) In the portrait of a girl in The 48 Hague, the pearl gleams just like her eyes – eyes and pearls have absorbed the earthly light and 55 glow with life and beauty. – If pearls can be the embodiment of earthly, transient beauty, how are we to interpret the picture of the Last Judgement behind the *Lady weighing pearls*? Vermeer's symbolism is not hard to understand.

If the *Astronomer* and the *Geographer* are really pendants, then they personify heaven and earth. The same symbols are to be found in the *Allegory of Faith*; the globe at the feet of Faith, and a crystal, the celestial sphere, hanging from a blue ribbon above her head.[51] But the *Allegory of Faith* presents 83 difficulties due not to its content, but to its artistic conception. One could quote Paul Claudel, who was an enthusiastic admirer of the picture – a lone voice. This personification of Faith is a fat, female figure with large feet and hands, and a head like an Easter egg; she is tightly swathed in her silk Sunday-best dress, blue and white and very shiny. Her attitude is almost indecent. Jan Steen's *Drunken Woman* has exactly the same pose. In the *Allegory of Faith* the painting of the curtain and

82, 79, 56 the chair is wonderful, but we have already come across curtains drawn aside and chairs placed at
33, 34 an angle in Vermeer's earlier pictures.

In his later pictures Vermeer repeated motives used in his early period and they are characterized only by the absolutely cold scale of colours and the jagged painting of the draperies, and also by the angular construction which comes close to the artistic intentions of the Cubists. The Arenberg

80, 81 portrait of a young woman who looks like a Sibyl is akin to the portrait of a girl in The Hague,

76, 54 but the coldness and sharpness of the colouring and draperies reveal that it is a late work, of the

74 same period as the *Girl with a guitar* at Kenwood and the two pictures in the National Gallery,

78, 79 London.

In his last pictures Vermeer reached the logical conclusion of his artistic possibilities, especially

83 in the *Allegory of Faith*, which has few admirers. His other allegory, however, the *Allegory of Painting*,

56 painted six or seven years before, is perhaps his most popular picture.

Hultèn, Steneberg, Gowing and Van Gelder[52] have endeavoured to explain this allegory. Briefly summarized, the interpretation is as follows: the model is Clio, the Muse of history; on the table lie the emblems of three other Muses: the mask of Thalia, the Muse of Comedy; the bulky book of Polyhymnia, the Muse of sacred song; and the score of Euterpe, the Muse of flute-playing.

The painter is seated on a low stool and is painting on a canvas with a grey ground and slightly inclined, on which we can see a light preliminary sketch in white chalk; right from the beginning he is using the mahlstick; he is wearing a gala costume such as in all probability was never really worn; the painter has his back turned to the spectator, so that one cannot recognize him and he remains anonymous; even his palette and his colours are invisible and he shows only what it is impossible to conceal; nevertheless, if the Muse of history were to raise her eyes and turn only slightly

58 towards him, she would be able to see his face. – This Muse, the Muse of history, is very young, perennially young; in her right hand she holds, rather clumsily, the trumpet of Fame and in the crook of her left arm, pressed against her heart, the gleaming golden record of the events of this world. She is the daughter of the Titaness Mnemosyne, of Memory, who records and rejects. The Muse of history is not looking at the painter, but from beneath sleepily drooping eyelids at the mask of Comedy. The painter is sitting in front of a map of the Netherlands, the symbol of his home; he is depicting the laurel-wreath of his Muse, bluer than the wreath she is actually wearing. Aloof and unrecognizable, he sits on his stool, gazing up at the Muse and mindful of nothing except his work.

In the Spring of 1672 the King of France began his war of aggression against Holland. A few months earlier Vermeer had moved out of his roomy house on the market square, after letting it for six years to his quasi-namesake Johannes van der Meer, for an annual rent of 180 florins. The painter moved with his family into a smaller house on the Oude Langendijk. The French invasion began; the Marshals of the Roi Soleil occupied a considerable portion of the Netherlands; the atrocities committed by the French are recorded in eleven engravings by Romain de Hooghe, which are anticipations of Goya's *Desastres de la Guerra*. William III of Orange became head of the Republic, ordered the sluice-gates to be opened and saved the Province of Holland and Amsterdam from the enemy. France gained nothing by the peace of Nijmwegen, but Vermeer did not live to see the end of the war, for on 15 December 1675 he was buried in the Old Church of Delft. He left hardly anything to his widow and his eleven children, except twenty-nine pictures by his own hand, more than half of those that he ever painted. Not one of his pictures is a repetition of another and yet they all look alike. His art had only one melody – just like a nightingale or a lark only have their own.

Wherein lies the charm, the unusualness, the beauty of these pictures? They are nothing but momentary visions, first seen through the camera and then transferred in paint to the canvas. They are bright, friendly pictures; they appeal to us, because they teach our souls how to fly towards the white light.

We too can sometimes, but not often, contrive to see the untouched beauty of things, perhaps in an unwontedly early morning hour, when the world is still full of water pearls and golden sunlight. Certain things move us owing to their form and colour: a butterfly on the petal of a flower, a sheaf of corn in an empty field, a bird hovering on its wings in the blue sky, the play of a flame, sheep or clouds moving slowly along. But such impressions are never very strong or clear and they never last for long. The ability to perceive everywhere the unchanging, powerful, inexpressible charm of things is what makes an artist, and what made Vermeer. Anything served his purpose. A pile of trivial things, dark in front of bright; a few yellow patches amidst brown wood or grey tiles, gleaming in the way sparks of light dance over water; a tiny spot of red in the darkness, like the call of a bird in the woods; a little patch of gold contrasted with blue; shadows and light in the relief of draperies, like a hilly landscape – all these things moved him with the vigour of an experience and he was able to reproduce them all in a painting.

We are fascinated by his pictures as we are fascinated by a couple of roses in a vase: a slightly darker or lighter tone, a red which is just a little different, a shading off into yellow or ivory-white, which for reasons we cannot fathom goes to our hearts, a different movement of the petals of a flower and we succumb to their beauty. Why is it that, of two similar things, one moves us and the other does not? Why are we moved by Vermeer's cold pictures and not by the soulful works of his contemporaries? With works of art it is the same as with human beings: many are called, but few are chosen.

NOTES

1 "Vermeer, die meesterlyck betrad zijn pade." Vermeer at that time was not a master, if we are to judge from the one or two pictures that may be dated from this early period. Of Fabritius, Arnold Houbraken (in his biographies of Netherlandish painters, published in 1719, in which he does not even mention Vermeer) says: "His talent, which had barely begun to flourish, was suddenly extinguished."

2 De Monconys also visited Frans van Mieris, who offered him a picture for 600 florins, and Gerard Dou, who had a picture for which he asked 300 florins. Pieter van Slingelandt offered him a painting for 200 florins, but De Monconys did not want to pay more than 60 florins for it. He did not buy any of these pictures, nor did he visit Rembrandt. On the other hand, when Cosimo III de' Medici came to the Netherlands in 1668, before his accession to the throne, he visited Rembrandt, but not Vermeer.

3 The curious thing about this is that the picture was in the possession of a baker. Was it security for a debt? A few weeks after Vermeer's death his widow owed the baker Hendrick van Buyten 617 "Guilders" and 6 "Stivers" for bread, and the baker had two paintings by Vermeer in his possession as security.

4 This is a high estimate of its value. In the autumn of 1676 Jan Coelenbier, an art-dealer of Haarlem, levied a distraint on twenty-six pictures forming part of Vermeer's estate; this he did on behalf of a woman shopkeeper in Delft, to whom Catharina Vermeer owed 500 (or perhaps only 442) florins for the supply of foodstuffs. (It is highly probable that a number of other pictures, namely those from Vermeer's art-dealer's shop, were at that time still all together in his house on the Oude Langendijk; according to the inventory of his estate, there were twenty-one pictures in the shop, among them three by Carel Fabritius, two by Hoogstraten and one by Jacob Jordaens. I therefore assume that the distrained works were all by Vermeer's own hand.) 500 florins for twenty-six pictures is a very low price; but it must be remembered that this was in the middle of the war between Holland and France, during which works of art were not a good market. At that time, and even several decades later, the paintings of Hobbema, Hercules Seghers and even Rembrandt, fetched very bad prices. During the following century the most-esteemed works were those of Gerard Dou.

5 It is true that before this isolated voices had been raised in praise of Vermeer, but they had had no response – Reynolds (1781), Lebrun (1792), Gautier (1858). On the other hand, Bürger-Thoré had no feeling for the limitations of Vermeer's work and made a number of wrong attributions – e.g. the *Sleeping Servant-girl* (Valentiner 199–B, Esaias Boursse) with a forged Vermeer signature, which belonged to Bürger-Thoré and was published by him in 1866 as by Vermeer; and also numerous paintings by Vrel, Cornelis de Mann, Van der Burch, and De Hooch (e.g. Valentiner 20, 21, 32, 62, 70, 228 and 254), which were attributed by him to Vermeer. Bürger-Thoré owned a number of genuine Vermeer pictures and seems to have been quite ready to sell them as well as other pictures. For example, in 1868 he sold a Pieter de Hooch which he had purchased only two years before (Valentiner 53). Vermeer's *Pearl Necklace* (Plate 45) was bought by Bürger-Thoré in 1869, and by 1874 had already been sold to the Suermondt

collection in Aix-la-Chapelle (now in the museum at Berlin). In the auction-sale of his estate (Paris, 5 December 1892), there were still three paintings by Vermeer (Plates 39, 78 and 79). The so-called "Self-Portrait of Vermeer" owned by Bürger-Thoré came to the Porgès Collection in Paris before 1900 and was there recognized as by Cornelis de Man.

6 In the course of the same lectures he maintained that "*Adriaen van Ostade was much finer as regards lighting effects than Rembrandt, that idol of the talented and untalented daubers and sketchers*", and in conclusion Burckhardt mentioned "*two really great masters – Terborch and Metsu*".

7 In the same letter Van Gogh gives us his canonical law: "*A Greek statue, a peasant by Millet, a Dutch portrait, a nude by Courbet or Degas – beside the serene and elaborate perfection of these things, the works of the Primitives and the Japanese seem only written characters as compared with painting.*" But Van Gogh's taste and works were not of his own time; during his lifetime he sold only one of his pictures.

8 About 1596 a poor artisan in Amsterdam, who had learned to read the Bible in Hebrew and Greek, became convinced that Jesus Christ could only have been a man. He was accused of heresy; the Burgomaster of Amsterdam defended him and said that "on account of his opinions" the man had been excommunicated and the Church ought to be satisfied with that. "It is my belief," he said, "that the life of a man should not be dependent on theological subtleties." The painter Torrentius, a Rosicrucian, was sentenced in Haarlem in 1628 to twenty years' imprisonment for proven debauchery and atheistical doctrines which he refused to retract; but he was released after two years. (Brandt, *Histoire de la Réformation des Pays-bas*, vol. i.)

9 "*Galilei died in the year in which Newton was born. That was the Nativity of our modern era*" (Goethe). Galilei's Copernican dialogues appeared in the year in which Vermeer was born.

10 The expression "Baroque" has been deliberately avoided in this outline of Vermeer's background. The normal connotation of "Baroque" as "*surging movement of all forms, enhancement of dimensions, rhetoric, theatricality, pathos, pomp and violence, in contrast to everything that is simple and restrained*" is certainly not applicable to the art of Vermeer (no more than it is to that of Hobbema or even Velazquez, or to the works of some of the great writers of the period, such as Gracian, Larochefoucauld or Molière). The numerous religious and philosophical trends had their counterparts in art and literature: everywhere the liberated spirit found its own forms, by turning to Nature with its visual experiences, colourful reality and psychological nuances. The real Baroque style was the hidebound tradition of the period, developed out of the Renaissance and Mannerism, a "Counter-Reformation of art"; and it was this traditional movement that found continuation in the styles of the following centuries.

11 Similarly, local schools of painting arose in Italy as a result of the activity of visiting artists from other parts of the country: in Padua, thanks to Donatello; in Milan, thanks to Leonardo; in Rome, thanks to Michelangelo and Raphael.

12 The catalogues of Dutch and German museums call him *Johannes*; that of the National Gallery in Washington, *Jan*. To avoid being pedantic, we do not call him *Joannes* which is how he himself signed all documents, but *Johannes*, as the London National Gallery Catalogue of 1960 puts his name.

13 It would seem that at that time running a tavern and dealing in works of art were not incompatible. In the seventeenth century, for example, travelling dealers in works of art often exhibited their wares in taverns. On 16 March 1611, in an inn at Augsburg, Hainhofer and the painter Rottenhammer purchased for the Duke of Pomerania a number of pictures from Hans and Justus Sadeler of Venice ("Quellenschriften", new series VI, 106).

14 This is not unusual. Many Dutch artists lived by dealing in works of art; during the last ten years of his life, when he was producing his greatest works, even Rembrandt's income was mainly derived from his share of the proceeds of the sales of works of art and antiques in the shop opened by his wife and son. Good painters had to resort to other trades in cases of necessity: Hobbema became a customs official; Steen, during his stay in Delft, ran a brewery; and Esaias Boursse died as a leading seaman on a ship of the Dutch East Indies Company. Trading in works of art was the most suitable of all professions for making a seventeenth-century Dutch artist independent of the tastes and demands of the public.

15 At the time pictures were generally regarded as good investments, as can be deduced from a frequently quoted passage in John Evelyn's diary: "13 August 1641. Rotterdam ... where was their annual marte or faire, so furnished with pictures (especially landscapes and drolleries as they call those clownish representations) that I was amaz'd. Some I bought and sent into England. The reason of this store of pictures and their cheapness, proceeds from their want of land to employ their stock, so that it is an ordinary thing to find a common farmer lay out two or 3.000 £ in this comodity. Their houses are full of them and they vend them at their faires to very great gains."

16 A. Bredius in *Oud-Holland*, vol. XXVIII, 1910, p. 62; Swillens, p. 188, document No. 12.

17 *Oud-Holland*, vol. XXXIV, p. 92; Swillens, p. 28 f. It is strange that Vermeer, who had not been in Italy, was entrusted with the valuation of Italian pictures (rather than two other painters from Delft, Leonard Bramer and Cornelis de Man, who had spent some years in Italy in their youth and knew its art treasures). The reason is apparently that Vermeer was an art dealer and valuer *by profession.* – In his own estate there were no Italian paintings, but only Netherlandish ones, among them three by Carel Fabritius, two portraits by Hoogstraten, a Crucifixion by Jordaens and some anonymous landscapes and still lifes.

18 Dutch art-dealers of the seventeenth century were not distinguished for their honesty. In the *Hollandsche Spectator*, sixty years after Vermeer's death, art-dealers and their methods were compared with horse-dealers and their tricks; they were said to have sold "worthless trash and clumsy copies" as genuine paintings, baptizing them with the names of Dou, Brouwer and Teniers. As a result, Jan Pieterszoon Zomer, a well-known Amsterdam dealer of that period, was nicknamed "John the Baptist".

19 Swillens, document No. 8: two paintings; document No. 9: one painting (*The Painter's Studio*, Plate 56); document No. 15:

twenty-six paintings. *Altogether twenty-nine paintings.* Documents Nos. 10 and 11 refer to pictures formerly in Vermeer's possession, but not by his own hand.

20 When one does not know who an artist's teacher was, it is impossible to make guesses as to his identity. Who, for example, could ever deduce from Rembrandt's works that his teachers were Swanenburgh and Lastman? The natural guess would be Hercules Seghers. After all, Rembrandt overpainted two works of Seghers, a Landscape (Uffizi, No. 1303) and a Portrait (Bredius, No. 238) and he reworked one of his etchings (Hind, No. 266).

21 The assumption that Vermeer was a pupil of Carel Fabritius is based solely on the line in Arnold Bon's poem (quoted above on page 7). But this merely states that Vermeer ought to be considered the successor of Fabritius, and does not claim that he studied under him. Nevertheless, it is possible, even though it cannot be proved and is improbable, that Vermeer worked in the atelier of Carel Fabritius between 1652 and 1654. It is curious that no one has ever attempted to attribute to the young Vermeer the *Portrait of a Man praying* (in the Berlin Museum, No. 819A, "workshop of Carel Fabritius".)

22 Even if this still-life were only a fragment of a larger picture and the background was over-painted, which is very unlikely, the fact remains that the background dates from that time and is in accord with the taste of the time – the last years of the sixteenth century.

23 Very similar was his relationship to Cornelis de Man (born in Delft eleven years before Vermeer and active as a master in that city since 1642). There is undoubtedly an affinity between the works of the two masters, but one is justified in doubting the correctness of the usual assumption that the more gifted of the two artists influenced the less gifted. Cornelis de Man had developed his style and established his themes before Vermeer was old enough to make his first experiments in painting. – The influence of Pieter de Hooch on Vermeer would also seem to be obvious, but the questions of priority in the painting of the period have not by any means been cleared up. Pieter de Hooch was born in 1629, Hendrick van der Burch probably as early as 1614; it may well be that both Hooch and Vermeer borrowed motives from Van der Burch, Hooch first and Vermeer later. If Van der Burch's painting, *The Conferring of Degrees at the University of Leyden* (Amsterdam, Rijksmuseum), can be dated about 1650 instead of 1658, then it would be entitled to priority as regards the style leading to Vermeer. (The catalogue of the Rijksmuseum, 1956, p. 44, dates Van der Burch's *Conferring of Degrees at Leyden* about 1650, that is to say earlier than similar pictures by Pieter de Hooch, all painted after 1654.)

24 After obtaining a divorce from her husband, Maria Bolnes-Thin, Vermeer's mother-in-law, lived in Gouda from 1641 on with her two daughters, while her son remained with his father. During the divorce proceedings a maidservant had stated that she could not confirm the allegation made by her mistress that she had seen the latter lying naked on the floor after being thrown out of bed, with her husband standing threateningly above her, holding a stick in his hand. At the time of her parents' divorce Catharina Bolnes was a child of ten. She probably had nothing more to do with her father, whose brick-works became more and more burdened with debts, or with her brother Willem; but her mother was always ready to help her (Swillens, pp. 184, 186, 195).

25 Despite all its weaknesses, the picture is the masterpiece of a beginner. Hale, in particular, has stressed the fact that it is painted contrary to all the rules of technique, and contrary to all the laws of disposition of colours. – The picture is divided into two halves by a horizontal line, and into two triangles by a diagonal running from top right to bottom left; the darker colours are in the triangle on the left, the brighter in that on the right. The centre is stressed by the three hands close together. – of the chief figure Renoir says: "Despite the title, this woman looks as if she were the most honest of creatures. She is surrounded by two young men, one of whom lays his hand on her breast, so that we can see that she is a courtesan, a hand full of youth and colour, which stands out against the vivid, lemon-yellow corsage."

26 This draped barrier is of Italian origin; it occurs, for example, in the work of Strozzi. The colouring of the picture is also Italian rather than Dutch.

27 *Rembrandt*, 1924, p. 149. – Dresden, No. 1559: "Rembrandt, Self-portrait of the artist with his wife Saskia on his lap, painted about 1635".

28 Lecture delivered at the twelfth International Congress of Art Historians, Brussels, September 1930. A similar remark is made by A. B. De Vries, p. 20. – The musician in the *Bawd* (Plate 13) is wearing the same black costume slashed with white and the same cap as the *Painter in his Studio* (Plate 56), which was painted ten years later. This costume (called "Burgurdian") was probably one of the atelier properties.

29 There is a whole literature on the subject; see André Chastel, *Melancholia in the Sonnets of Lorenzo de' Medici*, Journal of the Warburg and Courtauld Institutes, VIII, 1945, pp. 61–67. Chastel discusses the motive of a seated figure with "cheek resting on the hand".

30 This painting, nowadays generally attributed to Cesar van Everdingen, was in Vermeer's possession, and he also made use of it in other works of his (Plates 34 and 78).

31 In a painting attributed to Otto van Veen (in the store-rooms of the Berlin museum, No. 652, *Venus and Amor*; Catalogue 1931, p. 634: "Netherlandish, about 1590"), there is a similar mask thrown away at the feet of the God of Love.

32 According to Swillens, the girl is not asleep, but is a *sorrowing girl*, who, awake but with eyes closed, is plunged in the melancholy of love.

33 Above the sleeping soldier in the *Watch at the Gate* by Carel Fabritius (dated 1654, Schwerin, Landesmuseum), is a relief showing a pig at the feet of St. Anthony, obviously a symbol of "the temptation of sensuality". – One could also imagine that the soldier in Fabritius' painting is sleeping off the effects of a drunken carousal; even Vermeer's *Sleeping girl* incurred the same suspicion: at the auction sale in Amsterdam on 16 May 1696, it was described as "A drunken girl, asleep at a table".

34 The figure of the girl washing the feet of the goddess in the *Diana* is in the lower right corner, intersected like one of the figures of Degas; in the left bottom corner, also intersected and forming a kind of counterpart to the girl, is a dog. – Mary, however, sitting at the feet of Christ (Luke, x, 38) is the "sinner" who, in the house of the Pharisee, washed the feet of Jesus with her tears, dried them with the hairs of her head, kissed them and anointed them with the ointment. "Now when the Pharisee which had bidden him, saw it, he spake within himself, saying, This man, if he were a prophet, would have known who and what manner of woman this is that toucheth him: for she is a sinner" (Luke, VII, 39). Of her we are also told (Luke, VII, 47): "Her sins, which are many, are forgiven, for she loved much."

35 Swillens, p. 93 f. The home for old people was demolished in 1661 and replaced by the building of the Guild of St. Luke; which is a point of reference for the dating of Vermeer's *Street in Delft*. (Plate 18.)

36 Cf. Goethe in the introduction to his *Theory of Colour:* "The eye has to thank light for its existence . . . Although it may seem rather strange, we maintain that the eye does not perceive any form, since *brightness, darkness and colour together* are the only things that make up the entity which distinguishes one object from another and the parts of an object from one another. And therefore we put together the visible world out of these three things and at the same time make painting thereby possible, which is able to reproduce on a panel a far more perfect visible world than the real world can ever be." And later on: "Colours are the deeds of light, its deeds and sufferings."

37 Swillens, p. 94.

38 In an auction at Amsterdam in 1696, three landscapes by Vermeer were put up for sale: the *View of Delft* (Plate 27), the *Street in Delft* (Plate 18), and another view of a street in Delft that has since disappeared.

39 What Schopenhauer said of portraits of human beings can also be applied to portraits of towns: "Take note, young man, that the portrait should not be a reflection in a mirror, a daguerreotype reproduces that far better. The portrait must be a lyric poem, through which a whole personality, with all its thoughts, feelings and desires, speaks" (Schopenhauer in a conversation with the painter Julius Hamel, 1856). – Interest in precise topographical views dates from the end of the fifteenth century. The year 1493 saw the publication of Hartmann Schedel's *Weltchronik* with views of all the large towns in beautiful woodcuts; in the same year the Mantuan ambassador in Venice was instructed to procure a view of Venice and wrote to the Duke that Gentile Bellini was prepared to revise with the pen a large drawing made by his father. – The interest in views of towns dates from comparatively modern times and has continued ever since; but despite this it is difficult to find a dozen masterpieces of this category, or to find even one that can vie with Vermeer's *Delft*. – About earlier Dutch town view paintings see W. Stechow *Dutch Landscape Painting* (Phaidon, 1966), p. 125, and figs. 93 and 253.

40 When the attention of Jozef Israels was drawn to the *View of Delft* in the Mauritshuis, he exclaimed: "Tell me, what is the name of the painter? Ah yes, I know it already, Van der Meer." In 1931 the picture was exhibited at the Royal Academy in London; Wilson Steer, the leading English landscape painter of the time, said that he just could not understand why people made such a fuss about this picture. (De Vries, p. 15; Gowing, p. 65.) – But Marcel Proust, who saw it twice – in the Hague, on the 18th October 1902, and then again in the exhibition at the Jeu de Paume in May 1921, six months before his death, – judged it differently and wrote: "I knew that I had seen the most beautiful painting in the world."

41 Letter to Edmund Burke, 14.8.1781 (*From the Correspondence of Burke*, London 1844, II, pp. 424 f.; Leslie & Taylor, *Reynolds*, 1865, II, p. 336; *Letters of Reynolds*, ed. F. W. Hilles, Cambridge 1929, p. 84).

42 Reynolds' camera obscura has been preserved and is now in the Science Museum, London. The picture, when viewed in the camera obscura, does not differ greatly from a colour photograph, and Friedländer was thus more or less right when he talked about "the paintings of Vermeer reminding one of photographs". But already Paul Claudel, in his *Introduction à la Peinture Hollandaise*, remarked that the effect of Vermeer's work could only be compared to the delicate and miraculous images seen in a *camera obscura* or the visions of the first daguerreotypes.

43 Hyatt Mayor, *The Photographic Eye*, in *Bulletin of the Metropolitan Museum*, New York 1946, V-I, p. 20; L. Gowing, *Vermeer*, 1952, pp. 23, 69, 70.

44 K. T. Parker, *Windsor Drawings, Holbein* (1945), p. 30, *Canaletto* (1948), p. 26. – H. Fritzsche, *Bernardo Bellotto*, 1936, pp. 180–198 (with bibliography). – On Leonardo's glass-table apparatus, see J. P. Richter, *The Literary Works of Leonardo da Vinci*, second edition, 1939, Vol. I, p. 317, No. 523. – For general information see: Joseph Meder, *Die Handzeichnung, ihre Technik und Entwicklung*, second edition, Vienna 1923, pp. 467–470 and 544–551. – Further very important information about the camera obscura in Count Francesco Algarotti's *Saggio sopra la Pittura*, Bologna 1762; English edition 1764, French and German 1769.

45 Gowing, *Vermeer*, pp. 69–70; Hale, *Vermeer*, p. 199. – In addition to the portable camera obscura with a vertical image (inverted from left to right, if not equipped with a mirror) and the larger camera with a horizontal image, there were also fixed cameras showing very large vertical images in a frame, i.e. just as a picture stands on the easel. A variation of this camera is now in the possession of the Altertumsverein at Mannheim.

46 Hyatt Mayor, *The Photographic Eye* (1946), p. 20.

47 Nietzsche's works, Karl Schlechta edition, 1956, III, p. 691. – A similar observation was made by Grillparzer: "On the other hand, for me the things of real life . . . had a casual, incoherent, shadowy nature, which only became a necessity with the aid of poetry."

48 In the second edition of his *Inleyding tot de Hooge Schoole der Schilderkonst* (Rotterdam 1678, p. 233), Rembrandt's pupil Samuel van Hoogstraten recommended "een wakkere pinseelstreek", a free brushwork, the strokes of which should not be blended and obliterated, because in that case everything would become tedious. Vermeer's manner can hardly have met with Hoogstraten's approval and he makes no mention of him.

49 When viewed against a light-coloured ground, an image remains for a long time on the retina, as a silhouette with coloured edges. Against a dark ground it partially disappears from view. – The omission of the middle tones results in a simplification of the image and thus contributes notably to its visibility. It may be assumed that Vermeer found precedents for this omission of the middle tones in Italian and Netherlandish coloured and chiaroscuro woodcuts (e.g. in those of Andrea Andreani, Hendrick Goltzius, Lievens, etc.), just as Manet, later on, studied Japanese coloured woodcuts when he began to omit the middle tones in his paintings.

50 The expression comes from Carl Neumann, *Rembrandt*, p. 371: "The setting back of the figures, the freeing of the foreground, so that the front of the picture remains empty, i.e. is filled with air."

51 The Salvator Mundi holds a crystal of this kind in his left hand in paintings by Previtali and Dürer.

52 J. G. van Gelder, *De Schilderkunst van Jan Vermeer*, Utrecht, 1958; Hans Sedlmayr, *Jan Vermeer, Der Ruhm der Malkunst* (in "Festschrift für Hans Jantzen") Berlin, 1951; reprinted as *Probleme der Interpretation*, Hamburg, 1958; Kurt Badt, *Modell und Maler von Jan Vermeer: Eine Streitschrift gegen Hans Sedlmayr*, Cologne, 1961; Werner Hager, *Vermeer, Die Malkunst*, Stuttgart, 1966.
Vermeer's Allegory seems to be based on a paragraph in Franciscus Junius *De Pictura Veterum*, Amsterdam 1637 (lib. I, § 9). Junius says that the artists ought to do what the poets have always done – invoke the Muses right at the inception of any work and ask for their help. "The first of the Muses is Cleo . . . which in Greek is κλειω, i.e. Fame." In the following sentences Junius explains that *Cleo* means to want something, *Euterpe*, to enjoy what one wanted; *Melpomene*, to persevere in one's idea; and so on.

PLATES

1. CHRIST IN THE HOUSE OF MARY AND MARTHA. About 1654. Edinburgh, National Gallery of Scotland.   [Cat. No. 1]

2. MARTHA. Detail from Plate 1

3. CHRIST. Detail from Plate 1

4. MARY. Detail from Plate 1

5. DIANA AND HER COMPANIONS. About 1655. The Hague, Mauritshuis [Cat. No. 2]

6. TWO NYMPHS. Detail from Plate 5

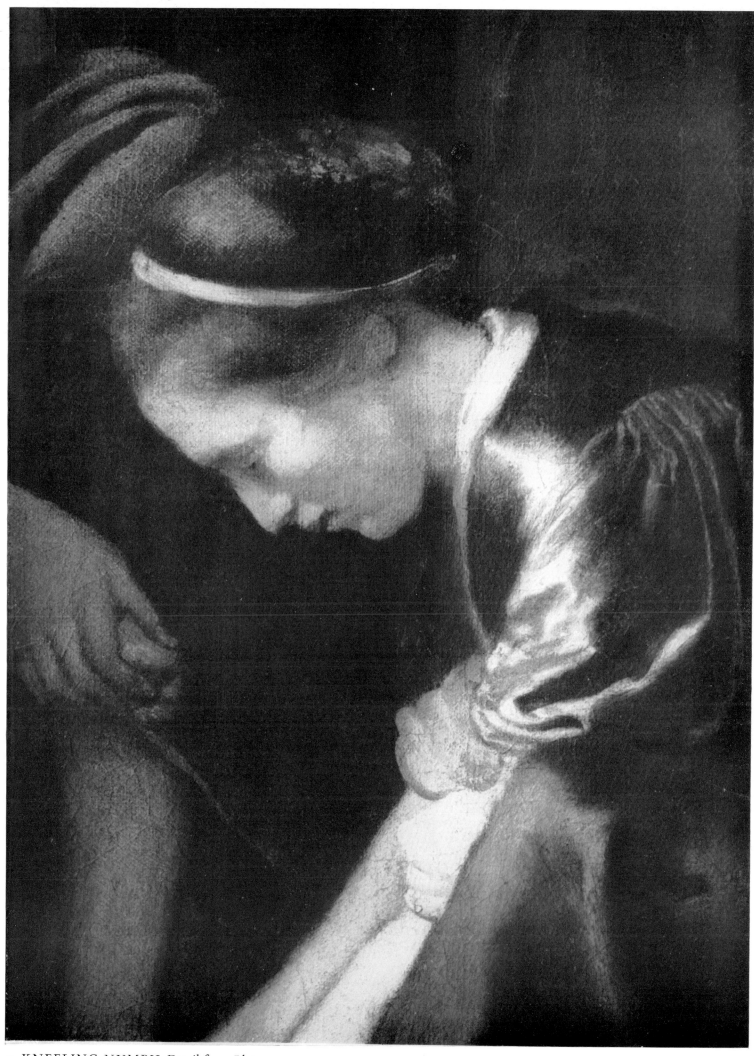

7. KNEELING NYMPH. Detail from Plate 5

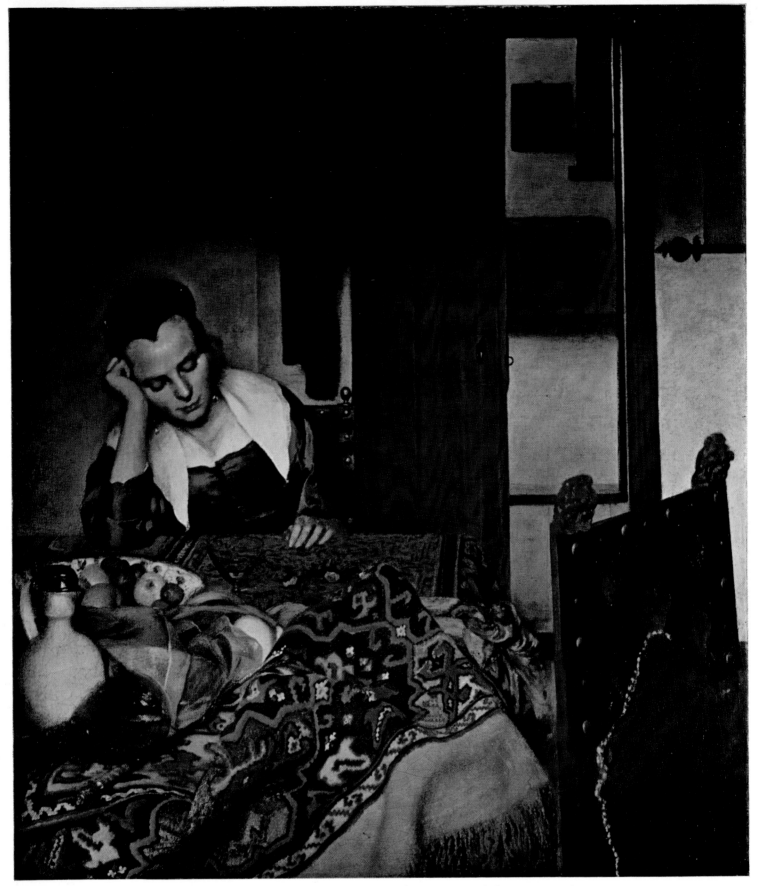

8. GIRL ASLEEP AT A TABLE. About 1656. New York, Metropolitan Museum (Altman Bequest)   [Cat. No. 3]

9. STILL LIFE. Detail from Plate 8, original size

10. HEAD OF SLEEPING GIRL. Detail from Plate 8, original size

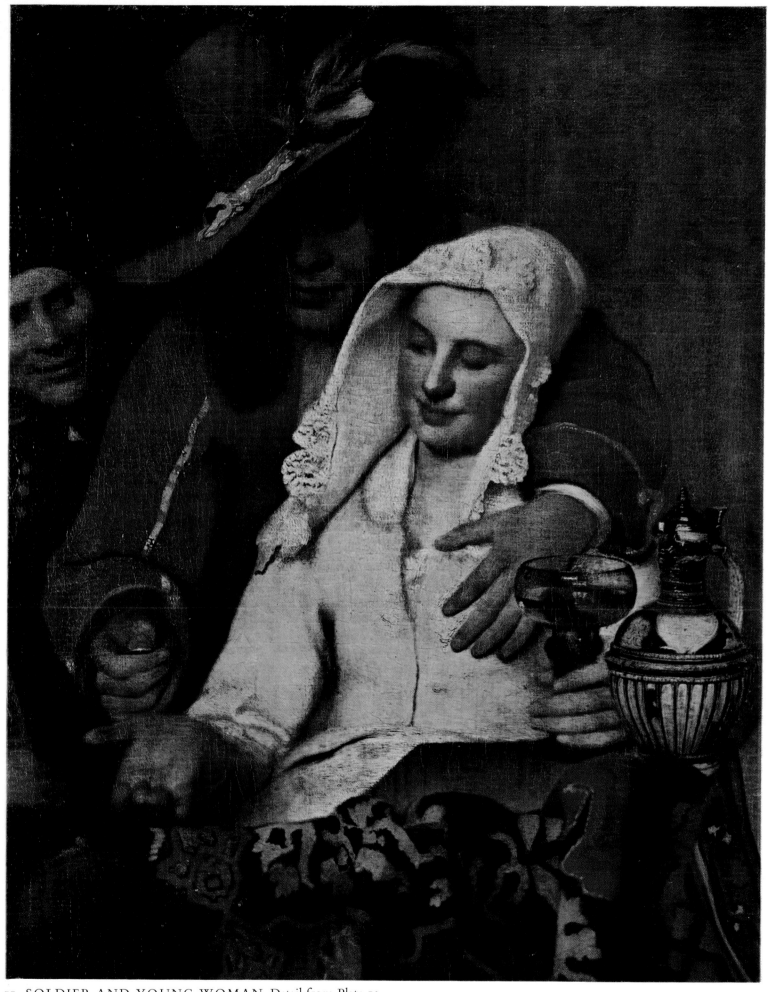

11. SOLDIER AND YOUNG WOMAN. Detail from Plate 13

12. MUSICIAN. (Self-portrait of the Artist?) Detail from Plate 13

13. AT THE PROCURESS. 1656. Dresden, Picture Gallery [Cat. No. 4]

14. SOLDIER AND LAUGHING GIRL. About 1657. New York, Frick Collection [Cat. No. 5]

15. LAUGHING GIRL. Detail from Plate 14, original size

16. LADY READING A LETTER AT AN OPEN WINDOW. About 1658. Dresden, Picture Gallery [Cat. No. 6]

17. LADY AND STILL LIFE. Detail from Plate 16, original size

18. A STREET IN DELFT. About 1659. Amsterdam, Rijksmuseum [Cat. No. 7]

19. HOUSES, A DOORWAY, AND A WOMAN. Detail from Plate 18

20. WOMAN SEWING AT AN OPEN DOOR. Detail from Plate 18, original size

21. MAIDSERVANT WARMING HER FEET. Drawing, original size. About 1659. Weimar, Museum   [Cat. No. 8]

22. HEAD OF A MAIDSERVANT. Detail from Plate 23, original size

23. MAIDSERVANT POURING MILK. About 1660. Amsterdam, Rijksmuseum   [Cat. No. 9]

24. STILL LIFE ON THE WALL. Detail from Plate 23, original size

25. STILL LIFE ON THE TABLE. Detail from Plate 23, original size

26. VIEW OF DELFT. Detail from Plate 27. About 1660. The Hague, Mauritshuis

[Cat. No. 10]

27. VIEW OF DELFT. About 1660. The Hague, Mauritshuis   [Cat. No. 10]

28. NEW CHURCH, CITY WALL AND ROTTERDAM GATE. Detail from Plate 27

29. OLD CHURCH AND QUAY. Detail from Plate 27

30. GIRL DRINKING WITH A GENTLEMAN. About 1660. Berlin, Museum   [Cat. No. 11]

31. GIRL DRINKING. Detail from Plate 30, original size

32. WINDOW. Detail from Plate 30, original size

33. TABLE AND CHAIR. Detail from Plate 30, original size

34. GIRL INTERRUPTED AT HER MUSIC. About 1661. New York, Frick Collection [Cat. No. 12]

35. THE MUSIC LESSON. Detail from Plate 38. About 1662. London, Buckingham Palace
Reproduced by gracious permission of Her Majesty the Queen

36. WINDOW. Detail from Plate 38

37. VIOLA DA GAMBA, AND TABLE CORNER WITH TURKEY CARPET. Detail from Plate 38

38. LADY AND GENTLEMAN AT THE VIRGINALS. About 1662. London, Buckingham Palace   [Cat. No. 13]
Reproduced by gracious permission of Her Majesty the Queen

39. THE CONCERT. About 1662. Boston, Isabella Stewart Gardner Museum [Cat. No. 14]

40. LADY AT THE VIRGINALS. Detail from Plate 39, original size

41. MAN ASLEEP AND STILL LIFE. Detail from Plate 42

42. THE COUPLE WITH A WINE GLASS. About 1663. Brunswick, Herzog Anton Ulrich Museum [Cat. No. 15]

43. WOMAN WITH A WATER-JUG. About 1663. New York, Metropolitan Museum (Marquand Gift) [Cat. No. 16]

44. WOMAN IN BLUE READING A LETTER. About 1664. Amsterdam, Rijksmuseum   [Cat. No. 17]

45. YOUNG LADY ADORNING HERSELF WITH A PEARL NECKLACE. About 1664. Berlin, Museum   [Cat. No. 18]

46. LADY WITH PEARL NECKLACE. Detail from Plate 45, original size

47. WOMAN IN BLUE. Detail from Plate 44, original size

48. LADY WITH A LUTE. About 1665. New York, Metropolitan Museum (Huntington Bequest)   [Cat. No. 19]
Before cleaning

49. LADY WITH A LUTE. Detail from Plate 46
After cleaning

50. LADY WRITING A LETTER. About 1665. New York, Mrs. Horace Havemeyer [Cat. No. 20]

51. LADY WEIGHING PEARLS. About 1665. Washington, National Gallery of Art (Widener Collection)　　　　　[Cat. No. 21]

52. LADY WEIGHING PEARLS. Detail from Plate 51, original size

53. THE LACEMAKER. About 1665. (Original size.) Paris, Louvre

54. HEAD OF A GIRL WITH PEARL EAR-DROPS. About 1665. The Hague, Mauritshuis [Cat. No. 23]

55. HEAD OF A GIRL. Detail from Plate 54

56. A PAINTER IN HIS STUDIO. About 1666. Vienna, Kunsthistorisches Museum [Cat. No. 24]

57. THE CHANDELIER. Detail from Plate 56, original size

58. THE MUSE. Detail from Plate 56

59. THE PAINTER. Detail from Plate 56

60. GIRL WITH A RED HAT. About 1667. (Original size.) Washington, National Gallery of Art (Mellon Collection)

[Cat. No. 25]

61. GIRL WITH A FLUTE. About 1667. (Original size.) Washington, National Gallery of Art (Widener Collection)
[Cat. No. 26]

62. THE ASTRONOMER. 1668. Paris, Private Collection   [Cat. No. 27]

63. THE GEOGRAPHER. 1669. Frankfurt, Staedel Institute   [Cat. No. 28]

64. HEAD OF THE GEOGRAPHER. Detail from Plate 63, original size

65. HEAD OF THE ASTRONOMER. Detail from Plate 62, original size

66. MAID HANDING A LETTER TO HER MISTRESS. About 1669. New York, Frick Collection   [Cat. No. 29]

67. HEAD OF A LADY. Detail from Plate 66, original size

68. SERVANT WITH A LETTER. Detail from Plate 66, original size

69. LADY WRITING A LETTER, WITH HER MAID. About 1670. Blessington, Ireland, Sir Alfred Beit, Bt.   [Cat. No. 30]

70. WINDOW AND CURTAIN. Detail from Plate 69

71. THE LOVE LETTER. About 1670. Amsterdam, Rijksmuseum [Cat. No. 31]

72. THE LOVE LETTER. Detail from Plate 71, original size

73. LADY WRITING. Detail from Plate 69

74. LADY WITH A GUITAR. About 1670. London, Kenwood, Iveagh Bequest [Cat. No. 32]

75. LADY AT THE VIRGINALS. About 1671. (Original size.) Blessington, Ireland, Sir Alfred Beit, Bt.   [Cat. No. 33]

76. HEAD OF A YOUNG WOMAN. About 1671. Palm Beach, Florida, Mr and Mrs Charles Wrightsman   [Cat. No. 34]

77. LADY SEATED AT THE VIRGINALS. Detail from Plate 79, original size

78. LADY STANDING AT THE VIRGINALS. About 1671. London, National Gallery   [Cat. No. 35]

79. LADY SEATED AT THE VIRGINALS. About 1671. London, National Gallery   [Cat. No. 36]

80. VIRGINALS AND CHAIR. Detail from Plate 78, original size

81. VIOLA DA GAMBA. Detail from Plate 79, original size

82. CORNER OF TAPESTRY. Detail from Plate 83

83. ALLEGORY OF THE FAITH. About 1672. New York, Metropolitan Museum (Friedsam Collection)   [Cat. No. 37]

84. CHALICE, CROWN OF THORNS, CRUCIFIX AND BIBLE. Detail from Plate 38

NOTES ON THE PLATES

VERMEER SIGNATURES

1: *Christ in the House of Mary and Martha*. Edinburgh (Plate 1). – **2**: *Diana and her Companions*. The Hague (Plate 5. This signature has almost completely disappeared). – **3**: *Girl asleep at a Table*. New York (Plate 8). – **4**: *At the Procuress*. Dresden (Plate 13). – **5**: not signed. – **6**: *Lady reading a Letter at an open Window*. Dresden (Plate 16. This signature has become very faint). – **7**: *A Street in Delft*. Amsterdam (Plate 18). – **8**: *Maidservant warming her Feet*, Drawing. Weimar (Plate 21). – **9**: not signed. – **10**: *View of Delft*. The Hague (Plate 27). – **11, 12**: not signed. – **13**: *Lady and Gentleman at the Virginals*. Buckingham Palace (Plate 38). – **14**: not signed. – **15**: *The Couple with a Wine-Glass*. Brunswick (Plate 41). – **16, 17**: not signed. – **18**: *Lady with a Lute*. New York (Plate 46). – **19**: *Young Lady adorning herself with a Pearl Necklace*. Berlin (Plate 48). – **20**: *Lady writing a Letter*. Mrs. Havemeyer Collection, New York (Plate 50). – **21**: not signed. – **22**: *The Lacemaker*. Paris (Plate 53). – **23**: *Head of a Girl with Pearl Ear-drops*. The Hague (Plate 54). – **24**: *A Painter in his Studio*. Vienna (Plate 56). – **25**: *Girl with a red Hat*. Washington (Plate 60). – **26**: not signed. – **27**: *The Astronomer*. Rothschild Collection, Paris (Plate 62. This signature is very doubtful). – **28**: *The Geographer*. Frankfurt (Plate 63. Inscription doubtful). – **29**: not signed. – **30**: *The Love Letter*. Amsterdam (Plate 69). – **31**: *Lady writing a Letter, with her Maid*. Beit Collection (Plate 71). – **32**: *Girl with a Guitar*. Kenwood (Plate 74). **33**: not signed. – **34**: *Head of a young Woman*. Wrightsman Collection, formerly Duc d'Arenberg (Plate 76). – **35**: *Lady standing at the Virginals*. London (Plate 78). – **36**: *Lady seated at the Virginals*. London (Plate 79). – **37**: not signed.

The figures refer to the Catalogue Nos. in the present book.

VERMEER SIGNATURES

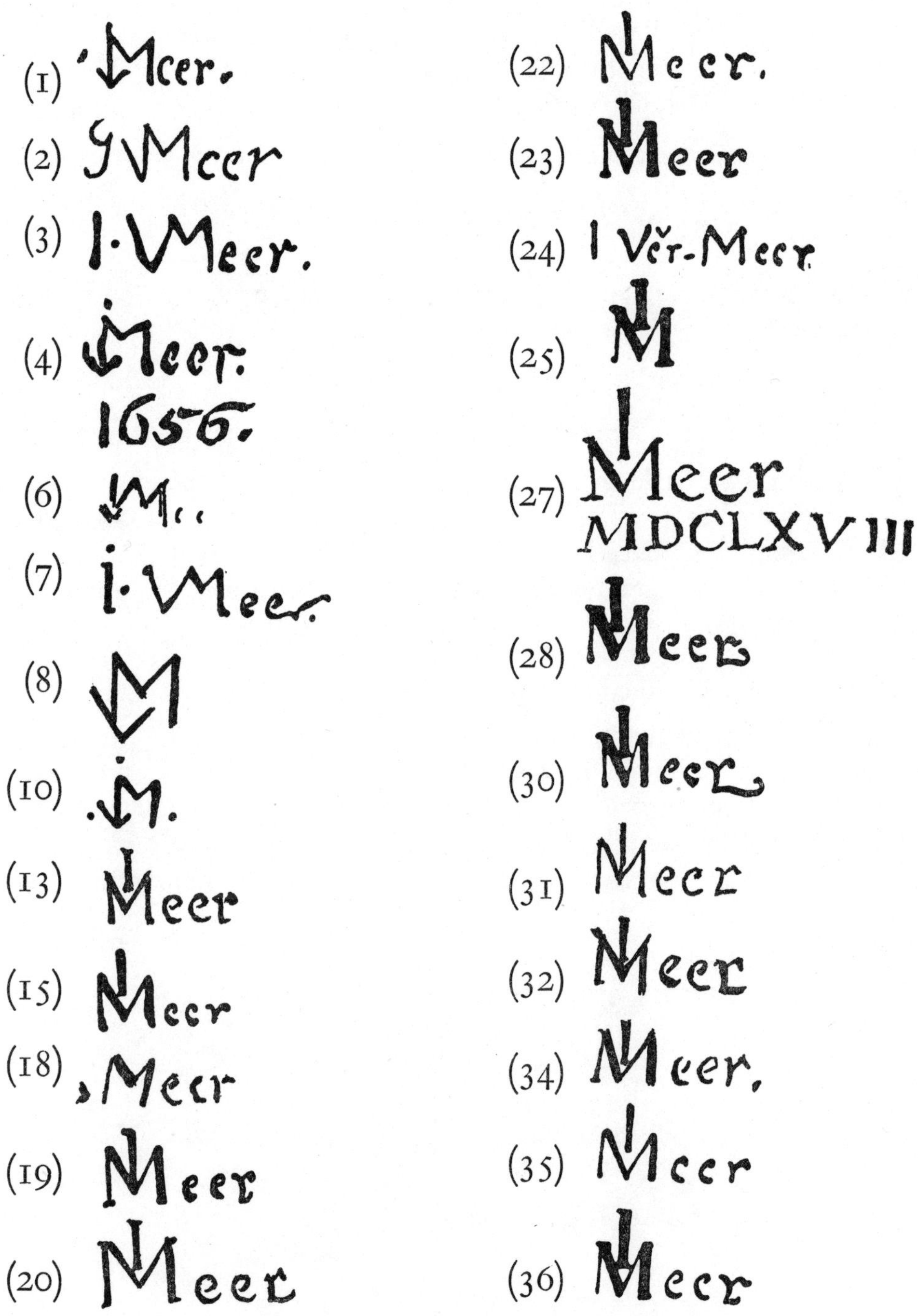

(1) Meer.

(2) JMeer

(3) I·VMeer.

(4) Meer.
1656.

(6) M..

(7) i·VMeer.

(8) M

(10) .M.

(13) Meer

(15) Meer

(18) Meer

(19) Meer

(20) Meer

(22) Meer.

(23) Meer

(24) I Ver·Meer

(25) M

(27) Meer
MDCLXVIII

(28) Meer

(30) Meer

(31) Meer

(32) Meer

(34) Meer.

(35) Meer

(36) Meer

The figures refer to the Catalogue Nos. in the present book.

NOTE

For the histories of the Vermeer paintings, i.e. their provenance, I have drawn on the Museum Catalogues and the books by Hofstede de Groot, De Vries and Hale; some additions contributed by Gowing are incorporated.

All known Vermeer signatures are reproduced here in facsimile on page 123.

Colour descriptions are given only of those paintings which are not illustrated here in full colour.

All Vermeer paintings are on canvas, with the exception of the *Girl with a Flute* in Washington (Plate 61), which is painted on a wooden panel.

The measurements are given in inches. (Measurements in cm. are added.)

The terms 'left' and 'right' refer to the left and right of the spectator.

The pages from Gerard Hoet's Catalogue concerning the Auction at Amsterdam, 16 May, 1696 (quoted in the present volume as "Amsterdam Auction, 1696") are reproduced in facsimile in Hale's *Vermeer*, 1937, as plates 54 and 55. Twenty-one items sold at this auction were pictures by Vermeer. A Dutch florin (or guilder) was the equivalent to about 16s. 6d. in English money at that time.

The following books are quoted in abbreviated form:

Gowing =*Vermeer*, by Lawrence Gowing. London, 1952.
Hale =*Vermeer*, by Philip L. Hale, new edition, completed and prepared for the press by Frederic W. Coburn and Ralph T. Hale. Boston, 1937.
Swillens =*Johannes Vermeer*, by P. T. A. Swillens. Utrecht, 1950.
De Vries =*Jan Vermeer van Delft*, by A. B. de Vries, new edition. London, 1948.

Vicenzo Catari: The Muses. Woodcut, 1615.

I

Plates 1–4

CHRIST IN THE HOUSE OF MARY AND MARTHA. About 1654. Edinburgh, National Gallery of Scotland. Signed on the stool, lower left corner. $63 \times 55\frac{3}{4}$ (160×142 cm.).

Bought by a furniture-dealer from a family in Bristol for £8. – Arthur Leslie Collection, London. – Art dealers Forbes & Paterson, London, 1901; there the signature was uncovered. – Bought by W. A. Coats, Skelmorlie Castle, Scotland. Presented by his two sons in 1927 to the National Gallery of Scotland, in memory of their father.

It has been pointed out that the figure of Christ is borrowed from a picture by Andrea Vaccaro (Naples, Pinacoteca Reggia di Capodimonte), or from a picture by Alessandro Allori (Vienna Museum), or from one by Erasmus Quellinus (at Valenciennes). In fact, this figure of Christ belongs to the repertory of Italian painters and was used in many studios in the 16th and 17th centuries; a detail from a Florentine painting of about 1640, by Giovanni Biliverti (Fig. 16), is shown here, just as a better example. (For a drawing by Fra Bartolomeo, with the same figure of Christ, see L. Münz, *Rembrandt Etchings*, 1952, Vol. II, p. 109.) The treatment of the drapery recalls the style of Jacob van Loo (cf. Fig. 1). The right hand of Christ was first painted in a slightly different position, and then re-painted by Vermeer; the index finger of the left hand has also been altered. As far as one can judge with the naked eye, the left arm and hand of Mary, part of her skirt and both feet, seem to have been retouched.

Swillens is the only critic who denies that this painting is by Jan Vermeer of Delft. His argument is in no way convincing. He ascribes the picture to Jan van der Meer of Utrecht, by whom there are two signed pictures in the Warsaw Museum (Inv. Nos. 131836 and 131837, dated 1656) – see Figs. 7 and 8.

2

Plates 5–7

DIANA AND HER COMPANIONS. About 1655. The Hague, Mauritshuis. Signed on the rock, lower left corner. The signature which has now disappeared (reproduced in the Museum Catalogue of 1895), stood probably for: J[oannes] R[eyniersz.] V[er] Meer. $38\frac{3}{4} \times 41\frac{3}{8}$ (98.5×105 cm.).

Art dealer Dirksen, The Hague (175 florins). – Neville D. Goldsmid Sale, Paris, 4 May, 1876, No. 68 (10.000 francs). Acquired by the Mauritshuis.

In the 1895 Catalogue of the Mauritshuis the painting was attributed to Jan van der Meer of Utrecht. Since 1907, when Bode accepted it without doubts, and Hofstede de Groot with some hesitation, as a work by Jan Vermeer of Delft, the picture has been fully recognized as such by all scholars, with the exception of Hale (1937) and Swillens (1950). Both made rather strange suggestions: Hale thought it could be by Anthonie Palamedesz; Swillens thought it might have been painted by Vermeer's father!

The picture has suffered a great deal from repeated cleaning and restoration. (Last cleaning in 1952.)

An influence of Jacob van Loo on this early work of Vermeer's is generally admitted (see Gowing, p. 96). Van Loo's *Diana*, dated 1648 and, according to Bode, the source of Vermeer's picture, has been destroyed by fire in 1945, together with other treasures of the Berlin Museum; a somewhat larger rendering of Van Loo's *Diana* still exists at the Brunswick Museum (No. 274, signed).

3

Plates 8–10

GIRL ASLEEP AT A TABLE. About 1656. New York, Metropolitan Museum. Signed at the left, over the head of the Girl. $34\frac{1}{8} \times 30\frac{1}{8}$ (86.5×76.5 cm.).

Amsterdam Auction, 1696, No. 8 (called "A drunken, sleeping girl at a table"; fl. 62). – John W. Wilson Sale, Paris, 1881. – Art dealer Charles Sedelmeyer, Paris, 1898. – Rodolphe Kann Collection, Paris. – Bought by Duveen Brothers, London, 1907. – Benjamin Altman Collection, New York, 1908; bequeathed by him to the Metropolitan Museum, 1913.

An influence of Nicolaes Maes on this picture is generally admitted. (According to Dr Hans Schneider, Maes stayed probably for some time at Delft in 1653 when he had left Rembrandt's studio in Antwerp and before he returned to his native Dordrecht.)

For the figure, with the head resting upon the right hand, compare Plates 4 and 42, and also Figs. 19 and 20; for the picture on the wall – usually ascribed to Cesar van Everdingen, and sometimes to Jan van Bronckhorst – see Plates 34 and 78; for the Turkish carpet compare Plate 4.

Hale (pp. 112–113) remarks that the picture has somewhat suffered from overcleaning, and also that "some painters who have examined it do not think it a Vermeer at all"; doubts which are hardly understandable.

4

Plates 13; 11, 12

AT THE PROCURESS. Dresden, Picture Gallery. Signed in the lower right corner and dated 1656. 56¼×51¼ (143×130 cm.).

One of the 268 pictures bought by the Dresden Gallery in 1741 from the Count Wallenstein Collection at Dux, on the advice of Carl Heinrich von Heinecken, author of "Nachrichten von Künstlern und Kunstsachen".

Ascribed until 1862 to Jan van der Meer of Utrecht; Swillens (1950, p. 155) lists it as a "doubtful attribution". Renoir admired this picture.

The areas of dark paint in this picture have cracked rather badly; the left hand of the Cavalier in red was first somewhat larger and was altered by Vermeer.

5

Plates 14–15

SOLDIER AND LAUGHING GIRL. About 1657. New York, Frick Collection. 19¾×17½ (49.2× 44.4 cm.).

Amsterdam Auction, 1696, No. 11 (fl. 44.10). – Mentioned in 1866 by Bürger-Thoré as in the Collection of Léopold Double, Paris, who had bought it in London for £246 15s. as a work by Pieter van Hooch. – Léopold Double Sale, Paris, 30 May, 1881. – Prince Demidoff Collection, San Donato, Florence. – Mrs. Samuel S. Joseph Collection, London. – Bought in 1911 by Henry Clay Frick.

The soldier wears a red coat with a black sash; the girl is in yellow and black, with a blue skirt. The table cloth is greenish, the map light brown and blue, the wall white, the frame of the opened window grey.

On the wall hangs a map of Holland and Friesland, inscribed NOVA ET ACCVRATA TOTIVS HOLLANDIÆ WESTFRISIÆ Q. TOPOGRAPHIA. The remainder is illegible. Swillens reads it: PER NICOLAVM PISCATOREM and ascribes the map to Nicolaes Visscher of Amsterdam (about 1618–1679). According to Louis A. Holman (quoted by Hale, p. 123, and pl. 17), this map is by the cartographer Willem Janszoon Blaeu (1571–1638) of Amsterdam.

The picture is painted at a short distance from the subject, the painter sat about six feet from the window (Swillens, p. 76). The window, the room and the chair are apparently the same as in Plate 16.

The picture has been cleaned in 1951.

6

Plates 16–17

LADY READING A LETTER AT AN OPEN WINDOW. About 1658. Dresden, Picture Gallery. Signed, on the right in the background, behind the girl. (Only a faint trace of this signature is left.) 33¾×25⅜ (83×64.5 cm.).

Bought in Paris for the Dresden Gallery in 1742 by the Legation Secretary of Saxony at Paris, De Brais, who died in the same year. Listed as Vermeer since 1862. (In 1783 it had been engraved as a work by Govert Flinck.)

The picture is rather dark in tone as the values of the blue paint have increased in the course of time. One characteristic of Vermeer's technique appears here for the first time: the manner of putting the paint on in small dry blobs, which is particularly apparent here in carpet and fruit.

7

Plates 18–20

A STREET IN DELFT. About 1659. Amsterdam, Rijksmuseum. Signed at the left under the window. 21⅜×17¼ (54.3×44 cm.).

Amsterdam Auction, 1696, No. 32 ("View of a House situated in Delft", fl. 72.10). – Auction G. W. Oosten de Bruyn, Amsterdam, 8 April, 1800. – Van Winter Collection, Amsterdam. – Six Collection, Amsterdam, until 1921. – Bought in 1921 by Sir Henry Deterding for fl. 680.000 and presented to the Rijksmuseum.

The picture is painted in small angular touches. The dark windows are brown on top of blue, the foliage yellow on top of blue. The yellow has faded and the foliage appears now rather blue; it is, however, possible that Vermeer had foreseen this effect.

The house on the right represents, according to Swillens, the Old Women's House in Delft, which was pulled down in 1661.

8

Plate 21

MAIDSERVANT WARMING HER FEET. About 1659. Weimar, Schlossmuseum. Drawing, reproduced here in original size. Signed on the "foot-warmer".

Since 1880 at Weimar.

The drawing is in black chalk, heightened with white, but parts of it are strengthened in red chalk, namely some of the outlines (the left hand and right side of the neck); red touches also on lips and cheek. The drawing is on bluish paper. The signature is very similar to the one on the *View of Delft* (Plate 27); this drawing must date from about the same time, or is a little earlier. It has still some resemblance to the Mary in the Edinburgh picture (Plate 1), even more to the little figure of a sewing woman in the *Street in Delft* (Plate 20), and, in parts, even to the *Milkmaid* (Plate 23).

H. Leporini (in *Stilentwicklung der Handzeichnung*, 1925, pl. 255) has reproduced this drawing as a characteristic work of Vermeer's; Swillens (p. 110) accepts it with some reservation.

9

Plates 23; 22, 24, 25

MAIDSERVANT POURING MILK. About 1660. Amsterdam, Rijksmuseum. 18×16¼ (45.4× 41 cm.).

Amsterdam Auction, 1696, No. 2 ("A maid pouring milk, exceptionally well painted", fl. 175). – Amsterdam Auction, 20 April, 1701, No. 7 (fl. 320). – Jacob van Hoek Sale, Amsterdam, 1719 (fl. 126). – Pieter Leendert de Neufville Sale, Amsterdam, 1765 (fl. 500). – Jan Jacob de Bruyn Sale, Amsterdam, 1798 (fl. 1550). – Hendrik Muilman Sale, Amsterdam, 12 April, 1813 (fl. 2125). – Bought by the Rijksmuseum in 1908 from the Jan Six Collection, Amsterdam (according to E. V. Lucas at a price of fl. 500.000).

Vermeer's "pointillé" manner is strongly pronounced in the rendering of basket and bread (cf. Plate 17). In the background at the right a footwarmer (cf. Plate 21). Reynolds, in his *Journey to Flanders and Holland*, 1781, mentions this picture as one of the best he has seen there. It still remains one of Vermeer's most popular pictures.

10

Plates 27; 26, 28, 29

VIEW OF DELFT. About 1660. The Hague, Mauritshuis. 38½×46 (98×117 cm.). Signed on the boat to the left.

Amsterdam Auction, 1696, No. 31 ("The town of Delft in perspective, seen from the South", fl. 200). – S. J. Stinstra

Sale, Amsterdam, 22 May, 1822, No. 112 (fl. 2900); bought by the Dutch Government.

In the foreground, on the right of the woman who is seen from the back, the figure of a man is faintly visible through overpaint. Here a figure had been painted, and was painted out again by Vermeer (a so-called *repentir*). There are *pointillés* on the boats, the bridge, and the foliage. The tone values of the blue paint have increased in the course of time, though only in the trees, where the yellow has faded, not in the roofs or in the water.

In the Städel Institute at Frankfurt, there is a drawing of a "View of Delft", bought for fl. 92 at the De Vos Sale, Amsterdam, 1833, and sometimes attributed to Vermeer. But, as already Swillens (p. 110) has pointed out, the paper of this drawing dates from the eighteenth century.

11

Plates 30–33

GIRL DRINKING WITH A GENTLEMAN. About 1660. Berlin, Museum. 26¼×30⅛ (66.3× 76.5 cm.).

Jan van Loo Sale, Delft, 18 July, 1736, No. 16 (fl. 52). – Collection of Lord Francis Pelham Clinton Hope, London, catalogued in 1891; bought in 1898 by Art dealer P. D. Colnaghi. – Acquired in 1901 by the Berlin Museum for £5000.

At the time of acquisition by the Museum the picture was heavily overpainted and was cleaned under the supervision of Bode and Friedländer; before cleaning there was, in place of the window, a view of a landscape. The picture has suffered a little from cleaning (e.g. the light edge of the bench, the back of the chair, and parts of the background; the right hand of the girl is retouched).

An earlier version of this picture exists in a private collection near Munich (Fig. 4). The perspective of tiles, table top, etc., is not as perfect as in the Berlin picture; it was probably painted by young Vermeer without the use of a camera obscura, and the figure is a later addition by Hendrick van der Burch. (See *Pantheon*, Munich 1964, pp. 35–38; and *Speculum Artis*, Zürich 1964, pp. 20–25.)

12

Plate 34

GIRL INTERRUPTED AT HER MUSIC. About 1661. New York, Frick Collection. 15¼×17¼ (38.7×43.9 cm.).

P. de Smeth van Alphen Sale, Amsterdam, 1 August, 1810, No. 57 (fl. 610). – H. Croese Sale, Amsterdam, 18 September, 1811, No. 45 (fl. 399). – C. S. Roos Sale, Amsterdam, 28 August, 1820, No. 64 (fl. 330). – Woodburn Collection. – Francis Gibson Collection, Saffron Walden. – Lewis Fry Collection, Bristol (1859). – Art dealers Lawrie & Co., London (1900). – Bought by Henry Clay Frick in 1901.

At one time the picture was badly overpainted; it was thoroughly cleaned in 1900, and again in 1949; the birdcage, according to Swillens a later addition, was not affected by the solvent.

The picture is on canvas (not on wood, as De Vries and Plietzsch say). The back of the chair, the cushion, the table cloth, the wine bottle, the cloak of the man, the skirt of the girl are painted in various shades of blue; even the music notes are in blue. The background varies from greyish blue to green. The jacket of the girl is of a warm red, and here and there in the painting is a little yellow.

13

Plates 38; 35–37

LADY AND GENTLEMAN AT THE VIRGINALS. (Also called *Lady at the Virginals and a Gentleman listening*; and also *The Music Lesson*.) About 1662. London, Buckingham Palace. Signed at the right, above the white jug, on the frame of the picture in the picture. 29×25¼ (73.6×64.1 cm.).

Amsterdam Auction, 1696, No. 6 ("A young Lady playing on the virginals in a room, and a Gentleman listening", fl. 80). – Bought from Consul Joseph Smith, Venice, in 1762 by Richard Dalton for King George III (as a work by Frans van Mieris).

On the lid of the virginals the inscription: MUSICA LETITIÆ CO[ME]S – MEDICINA DOLOR[VM] – (Music is the companion of joy, the cure of sorrows). The reading of the two words partly hidden by the lady's shoulder is uncertain; they have also been interpreted as CO[NSOR]S and DOLOR[IS]. The picture on the wall represents (according to Gowing, p. 123) "Roman Charity"; to judge from the small part one can see of it, it is in the style of Theodor van Baburen.

14

Plates 39–40

THE CONCERT. About 1662. Boston, Isabella Stewart Gardner Museum. 27¼×24¾ (69×63 cm.).

Baroness van Leyden Sale, Paris, 10 September, 1804, No. 62. – Christies Sale, London, 2 April, 1860, No. 49; bought by Art dealer Arthur Tooth, London. – Bought by Bürger-Thoré in 1886. – Bürger-Thoré Sale, Paris, 5 December, 1892, No. 31; bought by Mrs. Isabella Stewart Gardner for fr. 29.000.

This picture has sometimes been regarded as a counterpart to No. 13; this may be so, but the measurements of the two paintings are not the same.

The picture is in an indifferent state of preservation. The wall is grey, the tiled floor ivory white and black. The gentleman is in brown, with a sash in light brown; the back of his chair is orange. The dress of the seated lady is pale yellow, braided with black; the ribbon in her hair is pink. The standing lady wears a bluish green jacket and a blue skirt.

On the wall, towards the right, a painting by Theodor van Baburen, *The Procuress* (formerly in Vermeer's possession, now in the Museum of Fine Arts, Boston, signed and dated 1622; another version of Baburen's picture is in the Rijksmuseum, Amsterdam).

15

Plates 41–42

THE COUPLE WITH A WINE GLASS. About 1663. Brunswick, Herzog Anton Ulrich Museum. Signed on the glass of the window, right lower corner. 30¾×26½ (78×67.5 cm.).

From the Castle Salzdahlum near Wolfenbüttel, the Gallery of Duke Anton Ulrich (1710); in the Catalogue of the Salzdahlum Gallery of 1776; brought to the new Brunswick Gallery after 1813.

This picture is not in good condition. The face of the man, and the eyes, mouth and right hand of the woman are badly restored. The varnish has turned dark and too warm and ought to be removed.

16

Plate 43

WOMAN WITH WATER-JUG. About 1663. New York, Metropolitan Museum. 18×16½ (45.7×42 cm.).

Vernon Sale, London, 21 April, 1877 (as Metsu). Bought by Art dealer M. Colnaghi and sold to Lord Powerscourt, Powerscourt Castle, Enniskerry, near Dublin, Ireland. – Art dealers Bourgeois Frères, Paris, about 1880. – Art dealer Pillet, Paris, 1887; bought by Henry G. Marquand, New York, who presented it to the Metropolitan Museum in 1888.

The woman wears the same or a similar dress as the *Woman reading a Letter* at Dresden (Plate 17), but black is replaced here by blue. However, all the blue tones in this picture have turned stronger and independent, as for instance in the glass of the window, the shadow of the coif and the mapstick. Otherwise the painting is rather well preserved.

17

Plates 44 and 47

WOMAN IN BLUE READING A LETTER. About 1664. Amsterdam, Rijksmuseum. $18\frac{1}{4} \times 15\frac{3}{8}$ (46.5×39 cm.).

Pieter van der Lip Sale, Amsterdam, 14 June, 1712, No. 22 ("Woman reading in a Room, by Van der Meer van Delft", fl. 110. This could hardly refer to the picture in Dresden, Plate 16, which at that time was attributed to Govert Flinck.) – Pieter Lyonet Sale, Amsterdam, 11 April, 1791, No. 181 (fl. 43). – H. ten Kate Sale, Amsterdam, 10 June, 1801, No. 118 (fl. 110). – Paris Auction, 1809, fr. 95). – Lapeyrière Sale, Paris, 1825 (fr. 503). – Count de Sommariva Sale, Paris, 18 February, 1839. – Bought by Art dealers J. Smith & Sons, London, and sold for £70 to A. van der Hoop, Amsterdam, who bequeathed it in 1854 to the City of Amsterdam. Since 1885 in the Rijksmuseum.

This is the Vermeer painting that was admired by Van Gogh.

The covering of the chairs is painted in the same blue as the jacket but stronger in tone. On the table lies a brown cloth on top of a dark blue one.

18

Plates 45–46

YOUNG LADY ADORNING HERSELF WITH A PEARL NECKLACE. About 1665. Berlin, Museum. Signed at the table, $21\frac{1}{2} \times 17\frac{3}{4}$ (55×45 cm.).

Amsterdam Auction, 1696, No. 36 ("A young Woman adorning herself, very beautiful", fl. 30). – J. Caudri Sale, Amsterdam, 6 September, 1809, No. 42 (fl. 55). – D. Teengs Sale, Amsterdam, 24 April, 1811, No. 73 (fl. 36). – Henri Grévedon Collection. – Bürger-Thoré Collection, Paris, 1869. – Bought in 1874 by the Berlin Museum from the Collection of Barthold Suermondt in Aix-la-Chapelle.

The cloth on the table and the Chinese vase are dark blue; the tapestry on the chair is greenish blue and light brown, the chair in the foreground dark brown; the curtain is painted in the same yellow as the jacket, only a little stronger, casting a greenish blue shadow. This is one of the few Vermeer paintings in perfect condition.

19

Plates 48–49

LADY WITH A LUTE. About 1664. New York, Metropolitan Museum. Signed on the wall, beneath the table cloth (lower right corner in Plate 47). $20\frac{1}{2} \times 18$ (52×46 cm.).

From the Collection of Collis B. Huntington, New York, who had bought it in England, and who bequeathed in 1897 all his paintings to the Metropolitan Museum on certain conditions. He died in 1924, and in 1925 the Huntington Collection was transferred to the Metropolitan Museum.

This picture is less luminous than the others which I have dated from about 1664 (plates 44, 45); but Valentiner, De Vries, Trautscholdt and Gowing give it about the same date, 1663–64.

Apparently there is a *repentir* on the outline of the left arm of the lute player.

The picture has been cleaned in 1944; Plate 49 shows the present state, after removal of some overpaintings.

20

Plate 50

LADY WRITING A LETTER. About 1665. New York, Mrs Horace Havemeyer. Signed on the frame of the picture in the picture. $18\frac{1}{2} \times 14\frac{1}{2}$ (47×36.8 cm.).

Presumably Amsterdam Auction, 1696, No. 35 ("A young Lady writing, very good", fl. 63). – Presumably Dr. Luchtmans Sale, Rotterdam, 20 April, 1816, No. 90 (fl. 70). – H. Reydon Sale, Amsterdam, 5 April, 1827, No. 26. – Comte F. de Robiano Sale, Brussels, 1 May, 1837, No. 436 (fr. 400). – Bought in 1907 from a Paris art dealer by the Pierpont Morgan Collection. – Art dealers Knoedler & Co., New York. – Sir Harry Oakes Collection. – Lady Eunice Oakes Collection, Nassau. – Art dealers Knoedler & Co., New York, 1958.

Table cloth and jacket are apparently the same as in Plates 45–46, blue and yellow; but the wall is much darker, greenish grey, and the contrast of light and shade is considerably stronger here than in the soft and luminous Berlin picture. As in several other Vermeer paintings, the blue in the green shades has become stronger by age.

In the upper left corner a part of a picture is reproduced, representing a Still-Life with musical instruments (according to Isarlo in the style of Evaristo Baschenis, according to Boström by Cornelis van der Meulen). The inventory drawn up after Vermeer's death mentions, as hanging in the dining-room of his house, a still-life with "een bas met een dootshooft" (a viola da gamba and a skull).

21

Plates 51–52

LADY WEIGHING PEARLS (also called *The Gold Weigher*). About 1665. Washington, National Gallery of Art. 16½×14 (42×35.5 cm.).

Amsterdam Auction, 16 May, 1696, No. 1 ("A young lady weighing gold, a picture in a box, by J. van der Meer van Delft, very artistically and powerfully painted," fl. 155). – Amsterdam Auction, 20 April, 1701, No. 7 (fl. 113). – Nieuhoff Sale, Amsterdam, 14 April, 1777, No. 116 (fl. 235). – Collection of the Marquis de Caraman, French Ambassador at Vienna, who bought the picture at Munich (1826); his collection was sold after his return to France in a Paris Auction, 1830. – Casimir-Perier Sale, London, 1848 (bought in by his son for £141 15s.). – Collection of the Comtesse de Ségur-Perier, Paris (1910). – Art dealers P. & D. Colnaghi, London. – Philadelphia, Widener Collection.

The same blue table cloth as in Plates 45 and 50; the curtain is pale orange, the mirror in a black frame. On the wall hangs a picture of the "Last Judgement" (which looks like a later version of a famous composition by Jean Bellegambe).

22

Plate 53

THE LACEMAKER. About 1665. Paris, Louvre. Signed on the wall. 9½×8¼ (24.5×21 cm.)

Amsterdam Auction, 1696, No. 12 (fl. 28). – Jacob Crammer Simonsz. Sale, Amsterdam, 25 November, 1778, No. 17 (fl. 150). – J. Schepens Sale, Amsterdam, 21 January, 1811, No. 5. – H. Muilman Sale, 12 April, 1813, No. 97. (The *Maidservant pouring milk*, Plate 23, was sold in the same auction.) – Amsterdam Auction, 24 May, 1815 (fl. 9, sold to Gruyter). – Lapeyrière Sale, Paris, 14 April, 1817, No. 30. – Baron van Nagell tot Ampsen Sale, The Hague, 5 September, 1851, No. 40 (fl. 260). – D. Vis Blokhuyzen Collection, Rotterdam; sold at Paris, 1 April, 1870, No. 40 (fr. 7270); bought for the Collection of Napoleon III.

Most figures in Vermeer paintings are illuminated from the left; the exceptions are the present picture, the *Guitar Player* at Kenwood (Plate 74) and the two small Portraits in Washington (Plates 60 and 61). The tapestry on the table is apparently the same as in Plate 2.

23

Plates 54–55

HEAD OF A GIRL WITH PEARL EAR-DROPS. About 1665. The Hague, Mauritshuis. Signed in upper left corner. 18¼×15¾ (45×40 cm.). Probably not identical with No. 38 of the Amsterdam Auction, 1696: "A bust in antique dress, uncommonly artistic" (fl. 36). – Braam Auction, The Hague, 1882 (fl. 2.30, or about 4s. 6d.); bought by A. A. des Tombe, who presented the picture in 1903 to the Mauritshuis.

Not very well preserved; a hole under the left eye, cleverly restored, and another hole on the left cheekbone; and some other smaller damages. Some of the shadows in the dress are apparently retouched, and also some parts next to the left ear.

24

Plates 56–59

A PAINTER IN HIS STUDIO. About 1666. Vienna, Kunsthistorisches Museum. Signed on the map, behind the neck of the girl. 51¼×43¼ (130×110 cm.).

After Vermeer's death this picture was in the possession of his widow, who transferred it (24 February, 1676) to her mother as a security for a loan of fl. 1000; this amount Vermeer had borrowed from her in 1675. (Cf. Swillens, Document, No. 9, where the picture is called "De Schilderkonst".)

Probably not identical with No. 3 at the Amsterdam Auction, 1696 ("Portrait of Vermeer in a room with various accessories, uncommonly well painted by himself," fl. 45). – Baron Gottfried van Swieten Collection, Vienna. (Baron van Swieten, 1731–1803, the son of the famous Physician who came from Leiden to the Imperial Court, was Austrian Ambassador to Brussels, Paris and Berlin.) – Bought in 1813 by Johann Rudolf Count Czernin from a saddler for 50 Austrian Gulden as a work by Pieter de Hooch, whose name is inscribed on the rung of the stool. (This name has probably been added in a fraudulent way, at a time when De Hooch's name meant much more than Vermeer's; but the idea has also been advanced that De Hooch was the painter represented in this picture.) – In 1860 G. F. Waagen saw the painting in the Czernin Collection, recognized it as a work by Vermeer and also found his signature. – Until 1942 in the Czernin Collection (on loan to the Kunsthistorisches Museum, Vienna). From 1942 to 1945 the picture was in the possession of Adolf Hitler, who kept it at Berchtesgaden. – Returned by the Allies to the Vienna Museum (1946).

The painter in this picture is dressed in the same costume as the musician in Plate 13. The map (of the seventeen Provinces of the Netherlands) on the wall is inscribed: "NOVA XVII PROVINCIARUM . . . [. . .]A [. . .]ERI[. . .] RIS DESCRIPTIO . . . ET ACCURATA EARUNDEM [. . .] EDITA . . . PER NICOLAUM PISCATOREM".

(For Piscator or Visscher see Note on Plate 14.)

This map shows the Netherlands as they were under the Hapsburgs and must certainly date from before 1648. E. V. Lucas was the first to suggest that Vermeer's eldest daughter had been the model for the girl with book and trumpet; if this idea were accepted, the picture would have to be dated much later because Vermeer married in 1653 and his first two children were boys. Through the work of several scholars the meaning of this figure, which before had been called "Fama", has been clarified. As comparative examples for this earlier interpretation one could quote Federico Zuccari's drawing (in the Albertina, Vienna) showing his brother Taddeo working at a fresco and Fama with her trumpet hovering over him; or Pierre Mignard's Self-Portrait of about 1670, with Catherine Mignard dressed up as Fama, holding the canvas with the artist's portrait. Hultèn (1949) and J. G. van Gelder (1951) pointed out a similarity of the girl in Plate 56 to a "Muse Clio" in a painting by *Le Sueur*. This painting, datable 1647, now at the Louvre (No. 598), formed originally a part of the Hôtel Lambert decorations and shows a group of three Muses: Clio, Euterpe and Thalia. Gowing (pp. 139 f. and 142 f.) based his commentary on Van Gelder's idea: "*The model in the studio is Clio, and around her on the table lie the emblems of her sisters, the books of Polymnia and Euterpe, and Thalia's mask. Painting thus approaches Parnassus to take place with the ancient muses.*" (Compare Note 52, p. 33.)

In fact, since the time of Raphael, Clio was always represented in a similar way. A woodcut in the 1615 edition of Vicenzo Cartari's *Imagini* shows a Clio not very different from Le Sueur's. This woodcut is reproduced here (on p. 124) in reverse, to show its derivation from Raphael's *Parnassus*; Raphael's group of Muses can be studied best in Marcantonio Raimondi's engraving after the fresco (B.247).

The picture is not in perfect condition. Particularly the figure of "Clio" shows a number of retouches which become clearer in an enlarged photograph of the head: eye lashes, nostrils, the corners of the mouth are repainted. Some of the darker parts of the picture have also been tampered with by the restorer, probably in the 18th century.

(Plate 59 is not a colour reproduction; it is only one isolated attempt to reproduce, with two inks, as nearly as possible the richness of the gradation of tones in Vermeer's painting.)

25

Plate 60

GIRL WITH A RED HAT. About 1667. Washington, National Gallery of Art. Signed at the left above the hat. Reproduced in original size.

Lafontaine Sale, Paris, 1822. – General Baron Attahlin Collection, Colmar. – Sold by Baroness Laurent Attahlin to Art dealers Knoedler & Co., New York, 1925. – Andrew W. Mellon Collection. – National Gallery, Washington, 1937.

The authenticity of this picture is doubted by Van Thienen (1949), and by Swillens (1950) who gives no reason at all for his doubts. In fact, there are none; critics are still suffering from the Van Meegeren shock.

26

Plate 61

GIRL WITH A FLUTE. About 1667. Washington, National Gallery of Art. Reproduced in original size.

Jan Mahie van Boxtelen Liempde Collection, Hertogenbosch, Holland; in the Collection of his daughter, Maria de Grez, Brussels. – Jonkheer de Grez Collection, Brussels (where Bredius found it in 1906 and took it to the Mauritshuis for exhibition). – Art dealers J. Goudstikker, Amsterdam, and Knoedler & Co., New York. – Sold to Joseph E. Widener, Philadelphia.

This is Vermeer's only painting on wood; it is also the only one in which a figure is looking straight at us and not over her shoulder or away. Just as the head in Plate 60, it is illuminated from the right. The authenticity of the picture has been doubted, without sufficient reason, by Van Thienen and Swillens.

27

Plates 62 and 65

THE ASTRONOMER. Dated 1668. Paris, Private Collection. $19\frac{3}{4} \times 17\frac{3}{4}$ (50 × 45 cm.).

Rotterdam Auction, 27 April, 1713, No. 11 (fl. 300, together with the supposed counterpart, *The Geographer*, reproduced here as Plate 63). – Hendrick Sorgh Sale, Amsterdam, 28 March, 1720, No. 3 (fl. 160, together with No. 4: "A counterpart, by the same painter, as good"). – Govert Looten Sale, Amsterdam, 31 March, 1729, No. 6 (fl. 104, together with a counterpart). – Lebrun Collection, Paris (engraved reproduction of the picture in the

Catalogue of the Lebrun Gallery, 1792). – Danser Nijman Sale, Amsterdam, 16 August, 1797, No. 167 (fl. 132). – Jan Gildemeester Jansz. Sale, Amsterdam, 11 June, 1800, No. 139 (fl. 340, sold to Labouchère). – Christies Sale, London, 1863. – Léopold Double Sale, Paris, 30 May, 1881, No. 17. – Collection of Baron Alphonse de Rothschild, Paris, 1907; Baron Edouard de Rothschild Collection, Paris. – Exhibition "Chefs d'œuvre des collections françaises retrouvées en Allemagne", Paris, Musée de l'Orangerie, 1946.

The signature on the bookcase is very doubtful (see Swillens, pp. 58 and 176 f.); but this and the date may have been transferred from the original frame, when the picture was put into a new frame. The engraving in the Lebrun Catalogue (reversed reproduction of *The Astronomer*) shows no indication of a signature.

It has been stated that the picture is cut on the right; but this statement is only due to the fact that all previous reproductions were not quite complete. A seventeenth century copy of the picture in the Victor and Flora Koch Collection, London, shows exactly the same parts of the chair and of the picture in the background representing *The Finding of Moses* (cf. Plate 69).

The astronomer is in blue; background in grey and brown; instruments and books are pale yellow and light brown; the tapestry on the table is blue, green and yellow (the same as in Plate 53).

No. 32. – Art dealer Charles Sedelmeyer, Paris; bought by the Frankfurter Kunstverein (1885).

The signature and the date on the wall are, according to the Museum Catalogue, not genuine. The signature on the cupboard, behind the head of the Geographer, is also rather doubtful. The Catalogue of the Pereire Sale, carefully mentioning all signatures, knows of no signature on Vermeer's *Geographer*; the etching by Deblois in the same catalogue, a reproduction of the *Geographer*, shows no trace of a signature. On the other hand, Bürger-Thoré mentioned the signature on the door of the cupboard (1866). Perhaps this signature had become faint by 1872 and was re-drawn.

In the Govert Looten Sale, 1729, the Städel picture and the one in the Rothschild Collection were sold together and called "Two Astrologers by the Delft van der Meer". Despite the map in the background it is not certain that the Frankfurt picture represents a Geographer, because the white sheet of paper in front of the savant is a map of the stars, and the globe on the cupboard is a celestial globe. It is also doubtful whether this picture forms a pair with the Rothschild *Astronomer*; Vermeer used quite often a canvas size of about 50×45 cm.; there are five more paintings by him with these measurements, and therefore the almost equal measurements of the two paintings do not prove them to be *pendants*.

28

Plates 63 and 64

THE GEOGRAPHER. Dated 1669. Frankfurt am Main, Städelsches Kunstinstitut. 20⅞×18¼ (53× 46.6 cm.).

Supposed to be the counterpart of No. 27 (Plate 62).

Rotterdam Auction, 27 April, 1713, No. 10 (fl. 300, together with *The Astronomer*, Plate 62). – Hendrik Sorgh Sale, Amsterdam, 28 March, 1720, No. 4 (fl. 160, "together with a counterpart"). – Govert Looten Sale, Amsterdam, 31 March, 1729, No. 6 (fl. 104, "together with a counterpart"). – Perhaps at the Crammer Simonsz. Sale, Amsterdam, 25 November, 1778, No. 20 (fl. 172). – Danser Nijman Sale, 16 August, 1797, No. 168 ("7 louis", or fl. 133). – Art dealer Charles Josi, Amsterdam, 1798. – De Lange Sale, Amsterdam, 1803 ("36 louis", or about fl. 720). – Jonkheer Goll van Frankenstein Sale, Amsterdam, 1 July, 1833, No. 47 (fl. 195; sold to Art dealer Nieuwenhuys). – In the 1860 Catalogue of the A. Dumont Collection, Cambrai. – Isaac Pereire Sale, Paris, 6 March, 1872, No. 132 (fr. 7200). – Max Kann Collection, Paris. – Collection of Prince Demidoff, San Donato, Florence; No. 1124 in the Sale of his pictures, Florence, 15 March, 1880. – Adolf Joseph Bosch Sale, Vienna, 18 April, 1885,

29

Plates 66–68

MAID HANDING A LETTER TO HER MISTRESS. About 1670. New York, Frick Collection. 34¼×30¾ (89.5×78.1 cm.).

Amsterdam Sale, 1696, No. 7 ("A young lady to whom a maid brings a letter," fl. 70). – Blondel de Gagny Sale, Paris, 1776 (attributed there to Terborch, fr. 3902). – Poullain Sale, Paris, 5 March, 1780, No. 40 (fr. 4550). – Lebrun Sale, Paris, 1809 (fr. 600). – Paillet Sale, Paris, 1818 (fr. 460). – Duchesse de Berri Sale, Paris, 4 April, 1837, No. 76 (attributed there to Terborch, fr. 405). – Dufour Collection, Marseille. – E. Secrétan Sale, Paris, 1 July, 1889, No. 139 (fr. 75.000). – Pavlovstoff Collection, St. Petersburg. – Art dealer Sulley, London, 1905. – James Simon Collection, Berlin (325.000 Mark). – Art dealers Duveen Brothers, New York, 1919. – Bought, in the same year, by Henry Clay Frick.

The picture was cleaned in 1953. What seemed to be traces of a Vermeer signature, near the top of the shadowed side of the large casket on the table, disappeared at the touch of the lightest solvent, indicating that they were a later addition.

The table cloth (blue, with a shade of green), the

jacket (yellow with white ermine), the brown box and inkstand on the table are the same as in Plate 50. The hair of the lady is greyish brown. The servant is dressed in about the same colours as the servant in Plate 72.

30

Plates 69, 70, 73

LADY WRITING A LETTER, WITH HER MAID. About 1670. Blessington, Ireland, Collection of Sir Alfred Beit, Bt. Signed on the table, underneath the lady's left arm. $28 \times 23\frac{1}{4}$ (71×59 cm.).

After the painter's death this picture was in the possession of his widow who ceded it, together with another one (Plate 74), to a baker for a debt of 617 florins. – Josua van Belle Sale, Rotterdam, 6 September, 1730, No. 92 ("A young lady seated, writing a letter, with her maid standing and waiting for it, by Van der Meer"; fl. 100). – Franco van Bleiswijk Collection, Delft. Inherited by Hendrik van Slingelandt, in 1734; mentioned in his Inventory, 6 September, 1761, No. 17, and valued at fl. 30. – Miller von Aichholz Collection, Vienna. – E. Secrétan Sale, 1 July, 1889, No. 140 (62.000 fr.). – Art dealer Charles Sedelmeyer, Paris ("Catalogue of 300 Paintings," 1898, No. 86). – Marinoni Collection, Paris. – Art dealer F. Kleinberger, Paris, who sold it to Sir Alfred Beit, the father of the present owner.

The heavy curtain at the right is dark green, the transparent curtain in front of the window a pale orangy yellow; the tiles a dark greyish blue and pink buff; the servant is dressed in brown with a blue apron; the chair is covered in blue.

The picture in the background, in the style of Jacob van Loo (according to De Vries), represents the *Finding of Moses* (cf. Plate 62).

31

Plates 71–72

THE LOVE LETTER. About 1670. Amsterdam, Rijksmuseum. Signed (see Plate 70). $17\frac{1}{4} \times 15\frac{1}{4}$ (44×38.5 cm.).

J. F. van Lennep Collection, Amsterdam. – Messchert van Vollenhoven Sale, Amsterdam, 29 March, 1892, No. 14 (fl. 41.000). – Bought by the Rijksmuseum in 1893.

In the Inventory drawn up after Vermeer's death, there are listed in the dining-room, amongst other objects: A large picture representing *Christ on the Cross*; a *Seascape*; seven ells of gilt leather on the wall. In the *Love Letter* the gilt leather panel appears behind the figures, and the Seascape is on the wall. In the

Allegory of the Faith (Plate 83), where the floor is covered with the same tiles as in Plate 71, we find also the same gilt leather panel, and here the picture of Christ on the Cross is reproduced hanging on the wall. It is almost certain that Vermeer painted both pictures in his dining-room.

The scene of the *Love Letter* is rather difficult to make out. The figures are seen through an open door, which is partly covered by a tapestry hanging in the front room; at the right a chair, of which only the upper part is visible, not the legs; at the left of the door a map with its stick and knob at the lower end. Behind the lady, at the right, in the farther room is a large columnated mantelpiece, of which only a small part can be seen.

32

Plate 74

GIRL WITH A GUITAR. About 1670. London, Kenwood, Iveagh Bequest. Signed on the lower end of the curtain. $20\frac{7}{8} \times 18\frac{1}{4}$ (53×46.3 cm.).

Ceded, together with another picture – see Note on Plate 69 – in 1676 by Vermeer's widow in payment of a debt. – The pictures reproduced as Plates 69 and 74 are probably of about the same date. – Amsterdam Auction, 1696, No. 4 (fl. 70). – In the Collection of W. Cowper-Temple, later Baron Mount-Temple, by 1871; passed to Hon. A. E. Ashley, 1888; bought from him by Art dealer Agnew, London; Earl of Iveagh, 1889.

The picture is in perfect condition, still on the original stretcher and not lined. An old copy is in the John G. Johnson Collection, Philadelphia (No. 497, $20\frac{3}{8} \times 17\frac{7}{8}$ inches).

33

Plate 75

LADY SEATED AT THE VIRGINALS. About 1671. Blessington, Ireland, Sir Alfred Beit, Bt. (Reproduced in original size.)

In the first edition of the present book (p. 5 and p. 144) I said that I was not quite certain about this picture, and that we had to await the result of cleaning (which at that time was imminent). In May 1959 I was allowed to study the cleaned picture at the premises of Marlborough Fine Arts Ltd., London. It is, without doubt, a work from Vermeer's own hand, and was accepted as genuine by Hofstede de Groot, Plietzsch, Hale, Bodkin, and now also by A. B. de Vries and L. Gowing.

34

Plate 76

HEAD OF A YOUNG WOMAN. About 1671. Palm Beach, Florida, U.S.A., Mr and Mrs Charles Wrightsman. Signed in the upper left corner. $17\frac{3}{4}\times$ $15\frac{3}{4}$ (45×40 cm.).

Bürger-Thoré described the picture under No. 35 in his Catalogue of the Collection of the Duc d'Arenberg, 1859. According to information received from the Metropolitan Museum, New York (where the picture was exhibited in 1955 and 1957) the *Head of a Young Woman* was acquired by Mr and Mrs Wrightsman directly from the Arenberg Collection (according to Van Gelder at a price of about £150,000) and has not been cleaned since they acquired it. The earlier provenance of the picture is unknown. It cannot be identical with No. 38 or No. 39 or No. 40 of the Amsterdam Auction of 1696 ("38. A bust in antique costume, uncommonly artistic, fl. 36"; – "39. Another Vermeer of the same type, fl. 17"; – "40. A counterpart by the same, fl. 17."). Nor is it identical with a "Head of a Young Girl" sold for 3 florins (or about 5s. 6d.) at the Dr Luchtmans Sale, 20 April, 1816, No. 92, which had different measurements.

This picture is usually dated much too early, namely from the same period as the Head in the Mauritshuis (Plate 54). The hard and almost abstract shapes of the drapery and the colouring of the picture bring it in one line with the two late paintings in London (Plates 78, 79).

35

Plates 78 and 80

LADY STANDING AT THE VIRGINALS. About 1671. London, National Gallery. Signed on the musical instrument (see Plate 80). 20×18 ($50.8\times$ 45.7 cm.).

[According to Bürger-Thoré, Amsterdam Auction, 11 July 1714, No. 12, fl. 55.] – Jan Danser Nijman Sale, Amsterdam, 16 August, 1797, No. 169 (fl. 19). – E. W. Lake Sale, 11 July, 1845, No. 5 (sold at Christies). – Edward Solly Sale, 8 May, 1847. – Madame Lacroix Collection, Paris. – Bürger-Thoré Sale, Paris, 5 December, 1892, No. 30. Bought through Art dealers Lawrie & Co. for the National Gallery (£2400).

For the "Cupid" on the wall compare Plates 8 and 34. For the window compare Plates 63, and even 14 and 16. This picture – just as the earlier ones – is apparently painted in the same room of his old house "Mechelen", which he left on 12 January 1672, and moved on 1 May – a few weeks before the outbreak of the war with France – to a house on the Oude Langendijk. This gives a clue to a date *ad quem* for this picture, Plate 78.

36

Plates 79 and 77, 81

LADY SEATED AT THE VIRGINALS. About 1671. London, National Gallery. Signed on the wall (see Plate 77). $20\frac{1}{4}\times18$ (51.4×45.7 cm.).

First published by Bürger-Thoré, 1866, as in the Collection of Graf Schönborn, Schloss Weißenstein, near Pommersfelden, Bavaria. – Count Schönborn Sale, Paris, 17 May, 1867. – Bürger-Thoré Sale, Paris, 5 December, 1892, No. 32 (fr. 25.000). – Art dealer T. Humphry Ward, London, 1894. – Art dealer Charles Sedelmeyer, Paris, 1898. – George Salting Collection, London; bequeathed by him to the National Gallery in 1910.

The two pictures reproduced as Plates 78 and 79 are most probably counterparts.

For the picture in the background see Note on Plate 39, Cat. No. 14.

37

Plates 82–84

ALLEGORY OF THE FAITH. About 1672. New York, Metropolitan Museum. $44\frac{1}{2}\times34\frac{1}{2}$ ($113\times$ 88 cm.).

Herman van Swol Sale, Amsterdam, 22 April, 1699, No. 25 ("A seated woman, with a second meaning, representing the New Testament, by Vermeer of Delft, powerfully and glowingly painted," fl. 400). – Amsterdam Auctions, 13 July, 1718 and 19 April, 1735. – David Ietswaart Sale, Amsterdam, 22 April, 1749, No. 152 (fl. 70). – Art dealer Wächtler, Berlin, 1899, who had purchased it in Vienna as a work by Eglon van der Neer; (according to Plietzsch, *Vermeer*, 1939, p. 57, the *Allegory of Faith* appears in the background of a Double Portrait, dated 1824 and painted by the Vienna painter F. Waldmüller). Sold by Wächtler to Dr Abraham Bredius, The Hague (lent by him to the Mauritshuis at the Hague, exhibited there from 1899 to 1928). – Art dealer F. Kleinberger, Paris. – Colonel M. Friedsam, New York, 1928; bequeathed by him to the Metropolitan Museum, 1931.

The literary source of this representation was first recognized by Dr A. J. Barnouw (in *Oud-Holland*, 1914, p. 59 f.); he referred to a passage in Dirck Pietersz.Pers's Dutch translation (1644) of Cesare Ripa's "Iconology", where the following description of the *Allegory of the Faith* can be found: "The Faith is represented by a seated Lady ... with a Chalice in her right hand, her left hand on a Book which lies on a firm Cornerstone, i.e. Christ, and her feet resting on the Earth. She is dressed in sky-blue, with a carmine over-dress. Under the corner-stone lies a crushed Snake, and Death with his arrows broken; nearby an Apple representing Sin. Behind the woman, suspended on a nail, is a Crown of Thorns which needs no explanation. In the background is a representation of Abraham who is about to sacrifice his Son."

Vermeer's painting does not tally in every detail with Ripa's suggestions for an Allegory of the Faith; but there is little doubt that Vermeer must have known Ripa's text in the Dutch translation.

The theme of this allegory points to the probability that Vermeer's painting dates from a time after the French army had invaded Holland in 1672; it was a religious war – Catholics against Protestants.

As this late picture, the *Allegory of Faith*, was not in the possession of the widow (1675), it was perhaps commissioned by a patron who might have given Ripa's description to Vermeer as a programme for the Allegory. Vermeer's style appears rather cramped here, although certain parts, such as the curtain and the glass ball, are brilliantly painted.

On the wall – instead of *The Sacrifice of Isaac* that Ripa suggests – hangs a *Crucifixion* painted by Jordaens, formerly in Vermeer's possession and kept in his dining-room; now in the Terningh Foundation, Antwerp. (See Note on Cat. No. 31.)

The lady's bodice, the table cloth, the cushion on the chair, and the cord on which the crystal ball hangs are blue; the gown of the lady is white satin; the large tapestry on the left (not looking Dutch but rather Slav) is green and brown, with a little red and a good deal of blue; it is studded with *pointillé* dots; the carpet under the feet of the figure is mainly brown; under the Bible a green scarf; behind the crucifix a gilt leather panel; ceiling and tiled floor are similar to those in the *Painter's Studio* (Plate 56).

SOME DRAWINGS AND PAINTINGS

ATTRIBUTED TO VERMEER

are illustrated and discussed

on the following pages

No. I. *The Geographer*. Drawing. Dresden, Print Room. (Attributed to Vermeer by Karl Woermann.)

No. II. *Sleeping Maidservant*. Drawing. Amsterdam, Private Collection. (Attributed to Vermeer by Van Regteren Altena.)

No. III. *The Minuet*. London, Gimpel Collection. (Exhibited in London, 1927, as a Vermeer.)

No. IV. *Portrait of a Woman in Dark Blue*. Budapest, Museum of Fine Arts. (Attributed to Vermeer by Bredius, Hofstede de Groot
Hale, Plietzsch, and Valentiner.)

No. V. *The Lacemaker*. Washington, National Gallery of Art. (Attributed to Vermeer by M. J. Friedländer, Bode, Valentiner and Hofstede de Groot.)

No. VI. *Girl in a blue dress and yellow cloak*. (Attributed to Vermeer by G. Glück, Hofstede de Groot, M. J. Friedländer, a.o.) Private Collection in Sweden.

No. VII. *Girl with a Blue Bow*. Glen Falls, N.Y., Mrs. Louis F. Hyde Collection. (Attributed to Vermeer by Borenius and Valentiner.)

No. VIII. *The Smiling Girl*. Washington. National Gallery of Art. (Attributed to Vermeer by Bode and Hofstede de Groot.)

No. IX. *Young Woman with a Blue Hat*. Castagnola-Lugano, Countess Margit Batthyany. (Attributed to Vermeer by Plietzsch.)

DRAWINGS AND PAINTINGS ATTRIBUTED
BY SOME CRITICS TO VERMEER

THIS is a very small selection. Of many other attempts to ascribe all kinds of paintings and drawings to Vermeer one can learn from the Vermeer monographs by E. Plietzsch (1939), Hale-Coburn (1937, p. 205 f.), De Vries (London, 1948, pp. 63 and 96), Swillens (1950, pp. 110 and 157). But Plietzsch and Hale have also listed a number of wrong pictures as genuine, whereas the Catalogues of Vermeer paintings by Gowing and De Vries tally with my list. I have not dealt at all with the falsifications, of which the best known is the Emmanus picture by Han van Meegeren, painted in 1937 and sold for 520.000 florins ($170.000) to the Rembrandt-Vereeniging, Amsterdam; now at the Boymans Museum, Rotterdam. There are three monographs on the Vermeer fakes: M. van Dantzig, *Johannes Vermeer, De "Emmausgangers" en de Critici*, Leiden-Amsterdam, 1947; and Dr P. B. Coremans: *Van Meegeren's faked Vermeers and De Hooghs*, London, 1949; Sepp Schüller, *Falsch oder echt? Der Fall van Meegeren*, Bonn, 1953.

No. I. THE GEOGRAPHER.
Pen and ink and wash on white paper, $8\frac{1}{2} \times 6\frac{7}{8}$ (21.4×17.5 cm.). Dresden, Print-Room.
Attributed by Hofstede de Groot to Rembrandt (No. 251) and by Professor Karl Woermann to Vermeer. Arthur M. Hind (in his *Catalogue of Dutch and Flemish Artists*, Vol. I, p. 51, London, 1915) took the attribution to Vermeer seriously: "The attribution is not one to be lightly thrown away." In my opinion, this drawing is by Nicolaes Maes. (Seymour Slive, 1965, ascribed the drawing to Rembrandt.)

No. II. SLEEPING MAIDSERVANT.
Red chalk on light-brown paper. $15\frac{1}{2} \times 17\frac{1}{2}$ (39.5×44.6 cm.). Amsterdam, Private Collection.
Reproduced by Professor J. Q. van Regteren Altena, Amsterdam, in his *Dutch Master Drawings of the Seventeenth Century*, London, 1949, pl. 43, and attributed, with some doubt, to Vermeer. Swillens (1950, p. 111, No. 7), referring to the reproduction in *Oud-Holland*, Vol. 48, p. 272, describes this drawing as related in type and technical treatment to the drawing at Weimar (reproduced here as Plate 21). The Amsterdam drawing shows, however, strong resemblance to the *Sleeping Maidservant* which was No. 34 in the Sale of the Bürger-Thoré Collection of paintings (Paris, 1892) and is reproduced in Valentiner's *Pieter de Hooch* as Plate 199B, correctly attributed there to Esaias Boursse (Bürger-Thoré attributed it wrongly to Vermeer). This drawing is, almost certainly, also by Esaias Boursse.

No. III. THE MINUET.
Canvas, $23 \times 17\frac{3}{4}$ (60×45 cm.), cut on all sides and lined. London, Gimpel Fils Art Gallery (Mr Peter Gimpel).
The picture comes from Skelmorlie Castle, the Collection of W. A. Coats. (From the same collection came Vermeer's *Christ in the House of Mary and Martha*, now at Edinburgh; our Plate 1.) In 1927 *The Minuet* was exhibited at the Royal Society of British Artists, London, as by Vermeer. It shows resemblances to the manner of Ludolph de Jongh, Jacob van Loo, and Hendrick van der Burch. To the latter it was attributed by Valentiner (*Pieter de Hooch*, KdK. XXXV, 1929, p. 245); if it were really by him, this could be used as an argument for the supposition that Vermeer was his pupil. Gowing observed that *The Minuet* has "points of resemblance to the *Diana*" (reproduced here as Plate 5). "It is not impossible that evidence might emerge which would enable us to connect *The Minuet* with the unknown *juvenilia* of Vermeer himself" (Gowing, p. 97).
The picture is not in a bad condition but it shows overpaintings; e.g. on the left sleeve of the man, the curtain behind his head, etc.

No. IV. PORTRAIT OF A WOMAN.
Canvas, $32\frac{1}{4} \times 25\frac{1}{2}$ (82×65 cm.). Budapest, Museum of Fine Art.
From the Count Esterházy Collection, Vienna; there already before 1812, and attributed to Rembrandt; acquired in 1865 by the Hungarian Government. Bredius was the first to attribute it to Vermeer. This attribution was accepted by Hofstede de Groot, Valentiner, Plietzsch, and others. De Vries (p. 64) attributes it now tentatively to Willem Drost.
The woman is dressed in blue, with a yellow rosette on the white collar, holding white gloves with faint yellow trimmings. The cap and the dress of the woman are about the same as in Barent Fabritius's *Portrait Group of the Helm Family*, dated 30 September, 1656 (Rijksmuseum, Amsterdam; cf. F. van Thienen, *Costume of the Western World: Holland, 1600–1660*, London, 1951, Plate 55). Judging from the costume, the Budapest portrait dates therefore from the same

time as Vermeer's *At the Procuress* (our Plate 13) which is very differently painted.

No. V. THE LACEMAKER. Canvas, $17\frac{1}{2}\times15\frac{3}{4}$ (44×40 cm.). Washington, National Gallery of Art.

The picture was discovered in a Private Collection at Bremen in 1926; it was exhibited in 1927 at the Berlin Museum and accepted as a Vermeer by M. J. Friedländer, and Bode; later on also by W. Martin, Valentiner and Hofstede de Groot. Bought by A. W. Mellon in 1928. Hale was the first to point out that it is a rather weak painting. Not accepted as a Vermeer by De Vries, Swillens, Gowing, and other critics.

The figure in yellow and white sits before a greyish background; in the right corner a pewter dish and a blue cushion banded with yellow.

No. VI. GIRL IN A BLUE DRESS AND YELLOW CLOAK. Canvas, $19\frac{1}{3}\times15\frac{1}{8}$ (48.5×38.5 cm.). Private Collection in Sweden. – Reproduced here for the first time.

The quality of this picture is no doubt higher than that of the other attributions listed here. It has been accepted as authentic by Hofstede de Groot (1930), Gustav Glück (Director of the Vienna Museum; 1930), M. J. Friedländer (1947), W. Martin (Director of the Mauritshuis), E. Plietzsch (1955), a.o. – André Malraux (*Vermeer de Delft*, Gallimard, Paris, 1952, p. 122) tries to identify the picture with No. 39 of the auction sale in Amsterdam, 16 May, 1696.

No. VII. GIRL WITH BLUE BOW. Canvas, $15\frac{3}{4}\times13\frac{3}{4}$ (40×35 cm.). Glen Falls, New York, Mrs Louis F. Hyde Collection.

The picture came to light in a Christie's Sale on 23 March, 1934, and sold for £504; accepted as a Vermeer by Frank Davis, Tancred Borenius and W. R. Valentiner; but not by De Vries, Swillens, Gowing and other critics. Art dealer D. Katz sold it to America. It has suffered badly from a restorer's hand; old photographs, taken before cleaning, show it to better advantage.

No. VIII. THE SMILING GIRL. Canvas, $15\frac{3}{4}\times12\frac{1}{4}$ (40×31 cm.). Washington, National Gallery of Art.

This picture was discovered in 1926 in a Private Collection at Berlin and sold, with a certificate by Bode, as an early work by Vermeer to A. W. Mellon. Hofstede de Groot accepted it as genuine (1930), but not De Vries, Swillens, Gowing and Vitale Bloch.

The figure is dressed in buff with a white collar and a blue scarf on the head; the background is greenish.

No. IX. YOUNG WOMAN WITH A BLUE HAT. Canvas, $9\frac{1}{4}\times8\frac{3}{8}$ (23.5×21.3 cm.). Castagnola, Switzerland, Countess Margit Batthyany.

Sold in 1930 as a Vermeer by Art dealer Paul Cassirer, Berlin, to Baron Heinrich Thyssen-Bornemisza; now in the Collection of his daughter.

Accepted by Plietzsch (*Vermeer*, Munich, 1939, pp. 29–30) as genuine; De Vries (p. 65) calls it "a fake". This picture cannot be identified with No. 38 of the 1696 Sale of Vermeer paintings at Amsterdam, *A Portrait in an antique costume* (sold for fl. 36), or No. 39 (with the same title, sold for fl. 17), or No. 40 (a counterpart of No. 39, sold at the same price).

Four other pictures sold in the same auction have not yet been found: No. 5. "*A Gentleman washing his hands, in a room with a view into another room, with pictures [on the wall]; skilful and unusual*" (fl. 95). No. 9. "*A gay company in a room; vigorously and well painted*" (fl. 73. – Sometimes wrongly identified with Plate 14, or with Plate 39). No. 10. "*An Interior with a lady, and a gentleman making music*" (fl. 81. – Sometimes wrongly identified with Plate 39, which shows a Trio). No. 33. "*A View of a few houses*" (fl. 48. – Hofstede de Groot, No. 49, argued that this lost painting must have been of a smaller size than the *Street in Delft*, now at the Rijksmuseum, which fetched in the same auction a higher price, namely fl. 72.10).

BIBLIOGRAPHY

The following list is confined to the most important publications. Extensive bibliographies will be found in the appendices to the Vermeer monographs by Hale (1937), De Vries (1948) and Swillens (1950); also in Trautscholdt's article on Vermeer in Thieme-Becker's *Künstlerlexikon*, vol. 34 (1940) and in H. van Hall, *Repertorium voor der Geschiedenis Neder landsche. Schilder- en Graveerkunst* (first part, The Hague, 1936; second part, The Hague, 1949).

I. MONOGRAPHS AND ESSAYS
IN CHRONOLOGICAL ORDER

William Bürger (=Etienne Joseph Théophile Thoré): *Les Musées de Hollande*. Paris, 1858. – *Catalogue de la Galerie Suermondt* (Aachen), 1860. – *La Galerie d'Arenberg*, Brussels, 1869. – *Van der Meer de Delft*, in *Gazette des Beaux-Arts*, 1866, p. 297 f.; also in book-form: Paris, 1866; and a critical edition in German by Paul Prina, 1906. (See also A. Blum, *Vermeer et Thoré-Bürger*, Geneva, 1945, 2nd ed. 1946.)

Henry Havard, *L'état civil de Van der Meer de Delft*, in *Chroniques des Arts*, 1877, pp. 121–123.

Henry Havard, *Vermeer*, in *Gazette des Beaux-Arts*, 1883, p. 389 f.

Henry Havard, *Van der Meer de Delft*. Paris, 1888.

Cornelis Hofstede de Groot, *Jan Vermeer van Delft en Carel Fabritius*. With 42 photogravure plates in folio. Amsterdam, 1907. First supplement, 1913; second supplement, 1930.

Gustave Vanzype, *Vermeer van Delft*. Brussels, 1908. – New edition, 1921.

Eduard Plietzsch, *Vermeer van Delft*. Leipzig, 1911. New edition, Munich, 1939.

Philip Leslie Hale, *Jan Vermeer of Delft*. Boston 1913. – A new edition completed and prepared for the press by Frederick W. Coburn and Ralph T. Hale, Boston, 1937.

George Isarlo, *Vermeer à l'Exposition de Rotterdam*, in *La Renaissance*, October 1935.

René Huyghe, *Vermeer et Proust*, in *L'Amour de l'Art*, 1936, p. 7 f.

A. B. de Vries, *Jan Vermeer van Delft*. First edition in Dutch, Amsterdam, 1939; Revised German edition, Basel, 1945; English edition, London, 1948.

Thomas Bodkin and Ludwig Goldscheider, *The Paintings of Jan Vermeer*. London, 1940.

Elisabeth Neurdenburg, *Johannes Vermeer, eenige opmerkingen ooer Johannes Vermeer van Delft*, in *Oud-Holland*, LIX, 1942, pp. 65 f.; LXVI, 1951, pp. 34 f.

Benedict Nicolson, *Vermeer, Lady at the Virginals*. London, 1946.

Karl Gunnar Hultèn, *Zu Vermeers Atelierbild*, in *Konsthistorisk Tidskrift*, vol. XVIII, 1949, p. 90 f.

F. van Thienen, *Jan Vermeer*, London, 1949.

P. T. A. Swillens, *Johannes Vermeer, Painter of Delft*. Utrecht, 1950.

André Malraux, *Vermeer de Delft*. Paris, 1952. (With an introduction by Marcel Proust and quotations from Claudel, Gautier, Goncourt, Huizinga, Lhote, Renoir, Valéry, etc.)

Lawrence Gowing, *Vermeer*. London, 1952.

H. Gerson, *Het Tijdperk van Rembrandt en Vermeer*. Amsterdam, 1952.

Charles de Tolnay, *L'Atelier de Vermeer*, in *Gazette des Beaux-Arts*, XLI, 1943, pp. 265–272.

A. J. J. M. van Peer, *Drie collecties schilderijen van Jan Vermeer* in *Oud-Holland*, LXXII, 1957, p. 92 f.

J. G. van Gelder, *De Schilderkunst van Jan Vermeer*, Utrecht, 1958.

Kurt Badt, *Modell und Maler von Jan Vermeer*, Cologne, 1961.

II. THE DOCUMENTS

A number of documents relating to Vermeer were found in Dutch archives and published by F. D. O. Obreen (1877–1882), Abraham Bredius (1885–1910), L. G. N. Bouricus (1925) and A. C. Boogaard-Bosch (1939). They have been collected by Swillens, who quotes the original texts and gives a summary in English with bibliographical references in his monograph (1950, pp. 181–197). – The book containing the earliest mention of Vermeer's name is Dirck Evertsz. van Bleysweyck's *Beschrijvinge der Stadt Delft*, Delft, 1667, vol. II, 859, published by Arnold Bon; the latter's poem on the "Phoenix" is printed in the same volume on page 854. The frequently quoted statement by Balthazar de Monconys appears in his *Journal de voyage*, Lyons, 1666, vol. II, 149. For the auction sales see Gerard Hoet and P. Terwesten, *Catalogus of Naamlijst van Schilderijen met derzelven prijzen*, 2 vols., The Hague, 1752.

III. CHRONOLOGY

The older attempts have but little value nowadays, but we list at least the pioneers in this field: Jan Six, *Offizieller Bericht des Kunsthistorischen Kongresses zu Amsterdam*, 1896, p. 49; Theodor von Frimmel, in *Blätter für Gemäldekunde*, II, 1906, pp. 183–189; Wilhelm von Bode, *Rembrandt und seine Zeitgenossen*, 2nd. ed., 1907, p. 55; Cornelis Hofstede de Groot, *A Catalogue raisonné of the works of the most eminent Dutch Painters of the Seventeenth Century*, with the assistance of Dr. W. R. Valentiner, translated by E. G. Hawke, vol. I, London, 1907; Max Eisler, in *Vienna Yearbook*, XXXIII, 1916, pp. 213 f.; P. Johansen, *Jan Vermeer, A propos de l'ordre chronoolgique de ses tableaux*, in *Oud-Holland*, XXXVIII, 1920, pp. 185 f. – A chronology at variance with the others was proposed by W. R. Valentiner in *Pantheon*, X, 1932, pp. 305 f. – The following recent chronological attempts are notable and generally in agreement with one another: E. Trautscholdt in Thieme-Becker's *Künstlerlexikon* (1940, article on Vermeer); De Vries in the English edition of his monograph (1948); F. van Thienen in "A Tentative Chronology" (*Vermeer*, 1949); Lawrence Gowing in his *Vermeer* (1952), p. 78; and Vitale Bloch, *Tutta la Pittura di Vermeer di Delft*, Milan, 1954. – The chronology proposed by Jacob Rosenberg and Seymour Slive, in *Dutch Art and Architecture, 1600 to 1800*, London, 1966, is on the whole not very different from mine; but see the important note 5 on p. 271.

IV. ON VERMEER'S TECHNIQUE

Alfred Peltzer, *Über Malweise und Stil in der holländischen Kunst*. Heidelberg, 1943.

Jan Six, *De techniek van Vermeer etc.* in *Bulletin van den Nederlandschen Oudheidkundigen Bond*, second series, vol. I, 1908, and vol. II, 1909. – In the same periodical, C. F. de Wild on Vermeer's technique, vol. I, 1908, pp. 58 f., 156 f.

H. E. van Gelder, *Perspectieven bij Vermeer*, in *Kunst-historische Mededelingen van het Rijks-Bureau voor kunsthistorische documentatie*, The Hague, 1948-9.

Kjell Boström, *Peepshow or case*, in *Kunsthistorische Mededelingen*, 1949, pp. 21 f.

P. T. A. Swillens, *Johannes Vermeer*, 1950, pp. 113–140: *Technical Review*.

A. Hyatt Mayor, *The Photographic Eye*, in *Bulletin of the Metropolitan Museum of Art*, New York, new series, vol. V, No. 1, Summer 1946, pp. 15 f.

V. PERIOD AND STYLE

H. Floerke, *Studien zur niederländischen Kunst- und Kulturgeschichte*. Munich, 1905.

Wilhelm Dilthey, *Weltanschauung und Analyse des Menschen seit Renaissance und Reformation* (Gesammelte Schriften, Band II). Leipzig, 1914.

Max Eisler, *Alt-Delft, Kultur und Kunst*. Vienna, 1923.

J. Huizinga, *Holländische Kultur des 17. Jahrhunderts*, Jena, 1933.

W. R. Valentiner, *Pieter de Hooch*, Kd K. XXXV, Leipzig, 1939. (Discussing and illustrating also works by Hendrick van der Burch, Esaias Boursse, Ludolph de Jongh and Jacobus Vrel.)

Louis Gillet, *Les Tapis enchantés*. Paris, 1936.

Paul Claudel, *L'œil écoute*. Paris, 1946.

André Lhote, *Traité de la Figure*. Paris, 1950.

Etienne Gilson, *Painting and Reality*, New York, 1957 (pp. 27 and 79).

On the Netherlandish Caravaggists in the time of Vermeer:

Hermann Voss, *Vermeer van Delft und die Utrechter Schule*, in *Monatshefte für Kunstgeschichte*, V, 1912, pp. 79–83.

A. von Schneider, *Caravaggio und die Niederländer*. Marburg, 1933.

J. L. van Rijckevorsel, *Vermeer en Caravaggio*, in *Historia* IV, 1938-9, pp. 20–24.

Exhibition Catalogue: Caravaggio en de Nederlanden, Utrecht, 1950.

Paul Claudel, *Vom Wesen der holländischen Malerei* (pp. 32 f.), Vienna, 1937.

ACKNOWLEDGEMENTS

PRIVATE COLLECTIONS
Lord Chamberlain's Office, St. James's Palace, London
Sir Alfred Beit, Bt., Blessington, Co. Wicklow, Ireland
Mr. Peter Gimpel, London
Mrs. Horace Havemeyer, New York
Mr. and Mrs. Charles B. Wrightsman, Palm Beach, Florida

PUBLIC COLLECTIONS
Rijksmuseum, Amsterdam (Hr. A. Zettels)
Staatliche Museum, Berlin
Isabella Stewart Gardner Museum, Boston (Mr. George L. Stout)
Herzog Anton Ulrich Museum, Brunswick (Dr. Schmidt)
Museum of Fine Arts, Budapest (Dr. M. Aggházy)
Gemäldegalerie, Dresden (Verlag der Kunst)
National Gallery of Scotland, Edinburgh (Mr. Colin Thompson)
Städelsches Kunstinstitut, Frankfurt am Main (Dr. Schwarzweller and Dr. Voss)
Mauritshuis, The Hague (Hr. A. v. d. Vaart)
National Gallery, London
Iveagh Bequest, Kenwood, London County Council (Mr. A. L. Conran)
Metropolitan Museum, New York (Mr. Marshall B. Davidson, Miss Vera Andrus, Miss Nadia Hermos, Mrs. E. A. McGill and Dr. E. Winternitz)
Frick Collection, New York (Mr. Harry D. M. Grier and Miss Beatrice A. Magnuson)
Kunsthistorisches Museum, Vienna (Dr. E. M. Auer)
National Gallery of Art, Washington (Mr. Huntington Cairns, Mr. John Walker and Mrs. Fern Rusk Shapley)
Schlossmuseum, Weimar (Dr. Scheidig)

PHOTOGRAPHERS
R. Deegan, Dublin. A. Dingjan, The Hague. W. Dräyer, Zurich. Giraudon, Paris. Gabriele Hauck, Frankfurt, H. Heidersberger, Brunswick. Louis Held, Weimar. Percy Hennell, London. Lanièpce, Paris. K. Meyer, Vienna. W. Steinkopf, Berlin. Zoltan Wegner, London.

Thanks are due to Mr. Helmut Gernsheim for pointing out several errors in my concept of the history of the camera obscura.

INDEX OF COLLECTIONS

The numbers refer to the Plates